Bill Severn's
Magic in Four Acts

Bill Severn's
Magic in Four Acts

Bill Severn

Illustrated by Yukio Tashiro

STACKPOLE
BOOKS

Published by
STACKPOLE BOOKS
5067 Ritter Road
Mechanicsburg, PA 17055

Printed in the United States of America

10 9 8 7 6 5 4 3 2 1

Second paperback edition 1994 by Stackpole Books

Cover design by Kathleen Peters

Originally published in 1965
First paperback edition 1974 (David McKay Company, Inc.)

Library of Congress Cataloging-in-Publication Data

Severn, Bill.
    [Magic in four acts]
    Bill Severn's magic in four acts / Bill Severn ; illustrated by
Yukio Tashiro.
        p.   cm.
    Rev. ed. of: Magic shows you can give. 1965.
    ISBN 0-8117-2536-7
    1. Conjuring.   I. Severn, Bill. Magic shows you can give.
II. Title.   III. Title: Magic in four acts.
GV1547.S487   1994
793.8 — dc20   93-45672
                                                        CIP

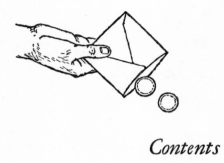

Contents

Introduction

THERE ARE many books of magic tricks, but this is one not just of tricks but of magic shows. Each show is complete, from the making of the things that are needed, through the talk that goes with them, to the final bows you will take when your friends applaud the fun you make for them with your magic. They have been planned to fit the place where they will be shown and the type of audience that will watch.

Here you will find shows to give at parties and clubs, as well as for scout, school, church and camp entertainments. They will take some learning, of course, and the amount of applause you get will depend on how well you perform them. But part of the fun is in the learning. With the shows all planned for you, there is no problem of wondering what to do next or of trying to think what to say.

If magic already is a hobby you enjoy, as hundreds of people do, you probably will want to change the shows around to suit your own way of performing. But it is hoped that even the advanced magic hobbyist may find some routines and ideas here that will add to the pleasure that comes from inviting audiences to pretend with him in the theater's oldest game of make-believe. The beginner will find nothing included that is really difficult to do or that requires expert sleight of hand. However, practice is needed, just as it is in learning a part in a play.

The charm of magic is in creating illusion. Fooling people and surprising them with happenings they don't expect is the role the magician plays. The tricks by themselves are far less important than the way in which they are presented. Professional magicians have proved time and again that the very simplest trick can entertain the wisest audience if it is well-presented. Every trick should be acted out, not just shown. The acts are here for you. All they need is someone to play the part of the magician. Someone like you.

Bill Severn's
Magic in Four Acts

ACT ONE

The Club Show

THIS IS the kind of a magic show you might give at any club meeting, dinner, scout or church gathering where you have been asked to entertain a group of about fifty people. Your audience may be a mixed one, including both men and women, and possibly some children. Since most club rooms are without stages, you probably will perform on a level with your audience and fairly close to those watching you.

It is a type of show that is less formal than one you would give on a stage. You can move freely into the audience and can call people up to take part in some of the routines. By "getting into the act," the audience feels closer to you. You can be more yourself, more easy-going and relaxed, than when you stand behind a barrier of footlights.

But it also has its drawbacks. Very often, you must set up your show with no curtain to keep everybody from watching you get it ready. You are limited in the use of big and showy props to help you play your role of magician. Sometimes the arrangements are such that the performing angles are poor for magic, and when you have finished, people may crowd around to investigate your secrets before you can put your props away. This act has been planned to meet most of those conditions, both good and bad, and detailed suggestions about setting things up for the performance will be found at the end of this section of the book.

When you are introduced as a magician, most people will look forward to seeing you do some of the tricks a magician usually does. To some extent, you should try to match the image of the magician they have in their minds and fulfill that expectation. Most of the tricks in this act are variations, either in theme or in method, of magical effects that have become classic, but with changes in their plots or stories to give them novelty. The basic appeal of their magic has been proven over the years and countless ways have been worked out to perform them.

They are the sort of tricks people expect a magician to do and the methods given should let you do them easily so you can concentrate on what is more important, the personality that you bring to them as you act the magician's part.

Under Your Spell

You start your show with a quick and colorful opening routine that provides a lot of small surprises while letting the audience get acquainted with you. It is one in which there is very little chance of anything going wrong, which is important not only because the success of your act depends on making a good first impression, but also because there is nothing for you to worry about. You can relax, smile, look out at the audience, let them see by your manner that you are about to give them a good show.

Showing a sheet of black paper empty, you form it into a tube and produce a colored silk handkerchief. As you talk about hypnotism in an amusing way, joking about whether you can put an audience under your spell, you push the handkerchief through the tube and it changes color. For a while, they think they have guessed part of the secret. But you surprise them by making a third handkerchief of still a different color magically appear. Showing the tube empty once more, you push the handkerchief into it and it transforms the three colors into a large rainbow-colored scarf.

The trick is self-contained. Its secret depends on the tube, which is made in such a way as to contain a concealed inner tube. This hides itself when you show the paper empty and curls itself back inside when you form the tube. As far as the working of it is concerned, all you have to do is fill the tube properly beforehand and then push the handkerchiefs in and take them out in the right order.

What you need:

Three Japanese silk handkerchiefs, yellow, blue and green, each 18″ square, and one multi-colored Japanese silk scarf, 24″ square. These are available in most variety stores.

An 18″ x 24″ sheet of flexible, but not too thin, black construction paper.

Black cotton binding tape.

White all-purpose glue, a yard stick, pencil, and a pair of scissors or a razor blade in a holder.

How you make the props:

From the black construction paper, cut one piece 9″ x 17″ and fold it vertically from left to right, like a book, so the two edges meet. Crease the fold flat. Next, from the original sheet of construction paper, cut a second piece 7″ x 7″. This second piece will form the hidden tube that will hold the handkerchiefs. You make it by first running a 1″ band of glue down the left edge. Now turn this sheet of paper over and press its glue-covered edge firmly to the center of the fold of the first piece of paper. Smooth it down, put a heavy book on it, and let it dry thoroughly.

When it is dry, smear another stripe of glue about 1″ wide down the left edge of this smaller sheet. Roll up this sheet from right to left to form a tube approximately 1½″ in diameter, sticking it firmly as it rolls on to the glue. Work your fingers or the yard stick inside the tube to make sure it sticks tightly and let it dry awhile.

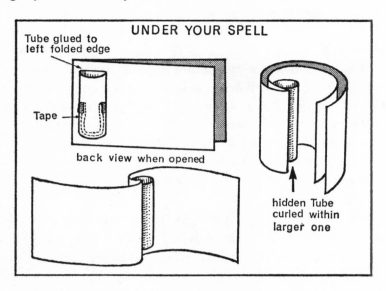

You now should have a tube glued to the center of the folded edge of the larger sheet of paper. With the scissors or razor blade, make two small slits in opposite sides of this tube at its center. Thread the black cotton tape through one slit and straight across and out the other. You will find this easier to do if you nip the end of the tape with the scissors and use them to pull it through. Adjust the tape until there is an equal length of it at each side. Push the center of the tape down within the tube to the bottom of it. Bend down what remains of the two upper ends of tape and glue them to the sides of the tube.

Finally, roll the still-folded big sheet of paper into a tube with the smaller tube inside it, and work your hands around it until the paper naturally curls in this position. To help give it a permanent curling, roll it tightly and snap some rubber bands around it. Keep the tube rolled up that way when it is not in use.

How you use them:

If you will hold the tube upright, so the two edges are to the right side, you will find that by taking one edge with your thumb and first finger of your left hand and the other edge in the same way with your right hand, you can simply draw your hands wide apart to show the tube empty. The secret inner tube automatically goes to the rear. Bring your hands together again and the tube curls itself up so the hidden one is inside it.

When you perform, the upright tube should be held chest-high, fairly close to your body, so you can turn a little to the right and left and let the whole audience have a clear view of the opened-out paper. Nobody must see the back of it, of course, but there is small danger of that unless someone is directly behind you.

Set this up for the routine by feeding the rainbow scarf into the top of the hidden tube and pushing it to the bottom so that the little sling of black tape goes down under it. Then put the green, yellow and blue handkerchiefs into the tube one at a time, in that order, on top of the rainbow scarf. Roll up the tube and snap a rubber band around it.

What you say and do:

MAGICIAN: Good evening.

(*Picks up tube and holds it upright. Removes rubber band and tosses that aside. Shows tube empty and allows it to close again. Holds closed tube in right hand and taps it smartly against open left palm. Blue handkerchief begins to appear as he finishes speaking.*)

It's fun sometimes, in this very practical old world of ours, to make believe there's such a thing as . . . magic!

(*Draws out blue handkerchief and displays it, shows tube empty and allows it to close again. Takes closed tube in left hand and holds handkerchief in right.*)

People ask me if magicians ever try to hypnotize their audiences to fool them. They don't, of course.

(*Starts pushing blue handkerchief slowly up into bottom of tube.*)

There's no way I could hypnotize you . . .

(*Smiles and makes a "hypnotic pass" at audience with right hand. Then continues to push blue handkerchief all the way up into the bottom of the tube until it is out of sight.*)

. . . into believing this blue handkerchief is becoming . . . yellow.

(*Removes yellow handkerchief from top of tube. Shows tube empty and allows it to close again. Displays yellow handkerchief with right hand.*)

You know perfectly well it's blue, don't you?

(*Reaches into bottom of tube with fingers of right hand and quickly pulls out blue handkerchief.*)

Or is it yellow?

(*Holds up one handkerchief and then the other.*)

Is it blue . . . or is it yellow . . . or were you hypnotized?

(*Holds both handkerchiefs in left hand with tube. Smiles at audience and snaps fingers of right hand as if breaking the "hypnotic spell." Takes both handkerchiefs in right hand and pushes them, one at a time, up into bottom of tube.*)

Anyhow, we all know that when you put blue and yellow together . . .

(Taps tube against left palm and then withdraws green handkerchief from top of tube as he finishes speaking.)

... you always get ... green!

(Displays green handkerchief. Shows tube empty and holds it open as he bows slightly, smiles and takes applause, as though trick were ended. Lets tube close again.)

Actually, this tube is an atomic color energizer. I know that sounds silly, but that's what it is. Blue ... yellow ... green ...

(Pushes green handkerchief up into bottom of tube.)

... put them all together and collect a few other colored atoms by magic ...

(With right hand, pretends to pluck a few "colored atoms" from the air and drop them into top of tube.)

... and what have you got?

(Makes a pass at the tube with right hand as if casting a spell.)

Why, a rainbow, of course!

(Produces rainbow scarf from tube and displays it. Shows tube empty. Bows and takes applause. Tosses tube and scarf into open suitcase on chair. Immediately begins talk for next routine.)

Fast and Slow

YOU HAVE put your audience in a receptive mood, shown something interesting and amusing, and have given people time to get acquainted with you. At this point, they should be thinking, "He seems like a nice fellow. There was nothing very startling about what he did, but it was fun. He's really pretty good at this—had me fooled with that one. I'll watch him more closely next time."

Now you can present something in a slightly more dramatic manner that will convince them their first impression was right. It will be a surprise that comes very quickly, capped by another in which the magic happens right before their eyes. You tell them you are about to show "the fastest trick in the world" and unless they watch closely, they'll miss it altogether. Tying together two white handkerchiefs, you put them in a cardboard folder so that the ends of both hang in plain view. You drop a separate white handkerchief into the folder with the two that are tied together. Before they can blink their eyes, you whip out the handkerchiefs and all three are tied in a chain, with the separate one firmly knotted between the others.

Then you say you'll do it in "slow motion," to show them exactly how the handkerchiefs managed to tie themselves into knots. You pick up another white handkerchief, tie a single knot in it and drop it on a tray, where it remains in full view. Then you untie one of the three handkerchiefs from the chain and put that one into the cardboard folder. Picking up the handkerchief with the knot in it, you hold it above the tray and the end creeps up and visibly passes through the knot to untie itself. You open the folder and the knot has passed to the other handkerchief.

Since this really is a combination of tricks, there are several secret devices involved. The first part of it, in which the single handkerchief becomes knotted between the other two, depends on the use of a handkerchief sewn together to form a bag so as to hide a duplicate which becomes part of the chain. This has long been a standard magical prop, used in an effect magicians call "The Twentieth Century Handkerchief Trick," in which a colored handkerchief vanishes and reappears. But here the effect is different and the handkerchiefs are all of the same color. This part of the routine also makes use of a specially prepared cardboard folder that conceals the first handkerchief in a hidden pocket.

The handkerchief that visibly unties its knot is worked by means of a short length of colorless nylon thread, fastened to the tray. The cardboard folder is again brought into use to switch the unknotted handkerchief for a knotted duplicate that is revealed at the end of the trick. This is accomplished by the design of the folder, which has a slit across half its double face, the slit being hidden by a strip of tape that forms part of the design. An unknotted handkerchief is put into the top of the closed folder and the knotted duplicate is pushed from its hiding place down through the slit so that when the folder is opened out flat it appears that the revealed handkerchief has knotted itself by magic.

What you need:

Six white Japanese silk handkerchiefs, each 18″ square.
Three pieces of white poster board, each 8″ x 10″.
All-purpose white glue.
A roll of ¾″ red cloth or plastic adhesive tape.
A spool of colorless nylon thread, sometimes known as "color blend" thread.
A small, rectangular metal tray, approximately 9″ x 14″.
Scotch tape, a pencil, ruler, and scissors or a razor blade in a holder.
You also will need the help of someone with a sewing machine who will sew one of the handkerchiefs into a bag for you.

How you make the props:

The handkerchief bag is made by first folding one of the handkerchiefs diagonally, so that its edges meet to form a triangle. Its edges then should be sewn together, except for a space of about 2″ that is left open at the top diagonal corner.

The folder is made in sections and then hinged together with red tape so it will open out flat like an office file folder. The red tape also is used to make decorative squares, one of which helps to conceal a secret opening in the face of it.

Start making this by putting one of the pieces of poster board on a table so its long edges are horizontal. Measure down 4″ from the top and about 1″ in from the left side and put a pencil dot there, then measure down 4″ from the top center and put another dot. Draw a line connecting the two dots. With razor or scissors, cut a slit along the length of the line.

Turn this piece over and on the back of it spread a patch of glue under the bottom edge of the slit. Now turn the piece face up again and put it on top of a second piece of poster board so all the edges exactly meet. Press it down so that the two pieces stick together beneath the slit.

Measure off 15″ of red tape. Fold back a 5″ length of this at the left end so the tape sticks to itself. You now have a length of tape that is sticky on the right half and doubled so that the left half of it is not sticky. Lay this horizontally across the middle of the poster board piece so that *the part of the tape that isn't sticky* comes directly over the slit and hides the opening. Run another strip of red tape vertically down the center of the card. The tapes make a design that divides the face of the card into four boxes.

With the red tape, bind together the two sides and bottom of the double card. Take another strip of red tape and run it along the top edge of *only the front part of the double card,* folding it over that edge to form a decorative border that will match the others at the sides and bottom. Trim the top edge of the rear piece of the card with a similar tape border.

The result should be a card of double thickness, with an opening at the top to the pocket formed between the two and a hidden slit half across the center. Take the remaining piece of poster board and put strips of red tape across it horizontally and vertically to form a boxed design that matches the other one and then bind the edges so they have a border that also matches.

With a horizontal strip of the red tape, hinge the bottom of the double card to the top of the single card so as to form a folder that will open out flat. Allow a tiny space between the cards when doing this so that the tape hinge will work freely. Reinforce the hinge by running a final strip all the way around, front and back.

You have now finished making the folder. The next prop to put together is the handkerchief that visibly unties itself. It is simply made by sewing one end of a 20″ length of the colorless nylon thread firmly to one corner of a handkerchief and then attaching the free end of the thread, just as firmly, under the back edge of the tray with a strip of transparent tape.

How you use them:

Before you put all the things together for the whole routine, it may be wise to try each of the props separately to understand how they work. Start with the folder, which incidentally may be used in many other tricks to make handkerchiefs appear, change or vanish. Hold it at the top with your left hand, fingers at the front and thumb at the back, so the folder hangs open. Bring your right hand up and shut the folder. Holding it with your left hand, pick up a handkerchief with your right hand. Tuck the handkerchief down into the secret pocket of the folder. Release the front of the folder from your left hand and it will fall open so that the handkerchief seems to have disappeared.

Now try something else with the folder. Take another handkerchief and tie a loose knot in its center. Fold the handkerchief on itself in small pleats to make a neat bundle and hide it inside the pocket of the folder directly above the slit. By holding your left fingers so as to press the top together, you can let the folder fall open and show both front and back of it. Close it again and pick up a second handkerchief. Push that one down into the secret pocket and, while your hand is still inside, thumb the other knotted handkerchief right out through the slit so it falls inside the closed folder. When you open the folder out flat like a tray, the knotted handkerchief will be seen. You have secretly exchanged one handkerchief for the other.

To try the handkerchief that visibly unties itself, use your left hand to pick it up from the tray by the corner that is opposite the thread. Hold it hanging a short distance above the tray. With your right hand, take the corner to which the thread is attached, bring it up and use both hands to tie a *large and very loose* knot in the handkerchief. Holding it above the tray with your left hand so the thread is taut, pull upwards very slowly and gently. The thread is invisible a few feet away. When the handkerchief has untied itself, let it drop from your fingers and fall back to the tray.

Set up the whole routine by starting with the threaded handkerchief. Put it on the tray so the threaded corner hangs over the back and the opposite corner hangs over the front. Place another plain handkerchief on the tray beside it, the diagonal corners of that also hanging over at the front and back in the same way. The next step is to load the folder. Tie a knot in the center of another handkerchief, fold it upon itself in small pleats, and tuck the bundle into the secret pocket of the folder at the side just above the slit. Shut the folder, turn it so the secret pocket is upwards and the hinge faces the audience, and place it on top of the handkerchiefs on the tray.

You fix the handkerchief that has been sewn into a bag by tying the corner where the opening is to the corner of another plain handkerchief and by then tucking that plain handkerchief down inside the bag until only 2″ of the corner

FAST and SLOW

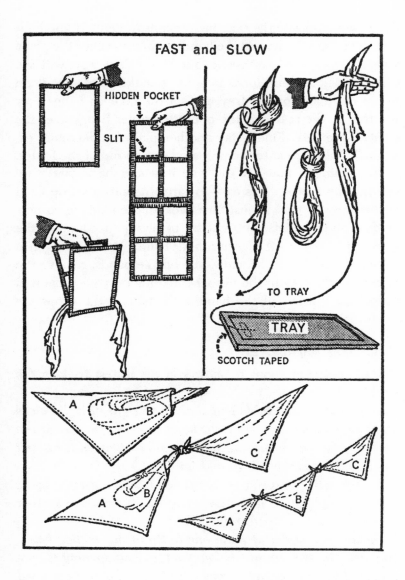

HIDDEN POCKET

SLIT

TO TRAY

TRAY

SCOTCH TAPED

A
B
C

diagonally opposite the tied one remains in view. If you hold your hand loosely around the handkerchief to cover the place where the exposed tip comes out of the bag, you will see that the whole thing looks like one handkerchief. Put it on top of the folder on the tray, so that the fake tip hangs over the tray to the rear and the opposite corner hangs over the front of the tray. Finally lay another plain handkerchief diagonally folded next to the prepared one on top of the folder.

Everything is now set the way it would be if you were starting the routine. It is easy to carry the entire set-up fixed in this way. To pack it, just turn back all the hanging corners of the handkerchiefs, put a sheet of newspaper around the tray and fasten it with large rubber bands. When you get to where you will give the show, slip off the bands, remove the paper, set the tray in the proper direction on your table and unfold the corners of the handkerchiefs, and the props are ready.

What you say and do:

MAGICIAN: I'm about to show you the fastest trick in the world.

(Standing behind table and slightly to right of it, he picks up bag handkerchief with right hand so his fingers cover the opening, then picks up the plain handkerchief with his left hand, and holds them high and far apart.)

In fact, it happens so fast that if you blink your eyes, you'll miss it completely. I'll tie these two handkerchiefs together by their tails . . . a good, tight knot.

(Really ties corner of plain one to tip of one in bag handkerchief. Holds them just below knot, so bag opening is concealed, and so they hang from raised right hand. Left hand picks up folder from tray and lets it fall open, back to audi-

*ence, holding it at top to keep secret pocket pressed shut.
Slowly turns left hand to show face of folder.)*

I have a little folder to put them in.

*(Right hand puts tied handkerchiefs into center of folder
so ends hang out each side. Closes folder and keeps it with
left hand. Right hand picks up plain handkerchief from tray,
tosses it into the air and catches it.)*

Another separate handkerchief.

*(Tucks it into top of folder, really down into left side of
secret pocket.)*

Two tied together . . . and the separate one on top.

(Holds folder high with left hand.)

Now, watch . . .

(Counts dramatically.) One . . . two . . . two and a half . . .

*(Reaches up suddenly with right hand. Firmly grasps the
corner of the nearest handkerchief and whips the chain of
three into the air with that hand as left hand lets folder fall
open.)*

The separate one . . . tied between!

*(Holds pose a moment. Smiles and bows, if applause, and
turns left hand to show back of folder.)*

I'll do it now in slow motion . . . to let you see how those
handkerchiefs tied themselves into knots.

*(Puts folder, hinge to audience, on table beside tray. Drops
chain of three handkerchiefs on top of it. With left hand,
takes the unthreaded corner of handkerchief remaining on
tray. Holds it above tray and lets it hang down to display it.)*

I'll tie a knot in this one over here.

*(Takes threaded corner with right hand and ties knot. Re-
moves right hand. Holds up handkerchief hanging down
from left hand to show it a moment. Opens left fingers and
lets handkerchief drop to tray.)*

And I'll leave this knotted one right here where you can see it.

(Picks up chain of three. Unties one handkerchief from chain. Discards others on table.)

This one has no knot.

(With left hand, picks up folder from table. Holds it at top to press pocket shut. Lets folder fall open. Turns left hand to show face of folder. With right hand, shuts folder.)

The one without the knot goes inside.

(Tucks unknotted handkerchief down into pocket of folder. While hand is still in pocket, pushes knotted one out through slit. Holds the closed folder with right hand. Steps back to right side of table.)

This is the knotted one . . .

(Left hand takes top corner of knotted silk, holds it above tray and keeps it there.)

. . . and this one is not knot . . . I mean, it has no knot.

(Nods to right hand that holds closed folder.)

Now . . . in slow motion . . . slowly . . . slowly . . .

(As he speaks, his left hand draws up slightly and gently and handkerchief visibly unties itself.)

. . . . while you watch.

(Holds pose a moment, then opens left fingers, lets handkerchief drop to tray.)

Meanwhile, the knot that now is not has tied itself into the handkerchief over here.

(Grips the ends of the folder with both hands and opens it out flat like a tray. Bounces the handkerchief into the air and catches it again on the flat folder. Lifts it with right hand and holds it high by one corner to show the knot. Drops folder to tray and slowly unties the knot.)

And that's the story of the little knot . . . that was fit to be tied.

The Little Black Bag

IF YOU have been playing your part of the magician well, the audience will be convinced by now that you can do some rather clever things. This is a good spot then for a change of pace in which your magic seems to go wrong. You stage a little situation comedy, leading those watching you to believe that they have caught on to one secret, then another, but you surprise them both times. Finally they are positive that they have guessed the truth, but the routine ends on a note of laughter when you prove them wrong again.

You start by introducing "one of the oldest tricks in magic," one you say they may have seen before, with a little black bag and a little white ball. The ball vanishes from the bag, then they think they see you hide it under your arm, but are wrong. It goes from your pocket to the bag and vice versa. When they guess you may be using two white balls, you confuse them by producing not two, but four.

Then you lead the audience into taking part in the trick by counting the balls with you as they vanish one at a time while being dropped through a paper tube into a basket.

They are sure the "vanished" balls are still concealed in the paper tube. But you crush the tube and toss it to them. It is empty, after all.

Part of the secret depends on the use of table tennis balls. Their light weight helps conceal them inside a double cloth bag. The rest of the routine is accomplished by using a half-ball, which looks like a whole one when you hold it facing front. It also looks like a single ball when another one falls inside it. Although the routine is an easy one to do as far as the magic is concerned, since it almost works itself, it will require practice. Its success depends on smoothness, pace, and most importantly, rehearsed acting and facial expressions.

What you need:

Once again, you will have to call on the services of someone who can do some machine sewing for you. For this, you will need three pieces of heavy black rayon lining material, each 9½″ x 11″.

Five white tennis balls.

A basket approximately 10″ in diameter and 4″ deep. This should be the tightly woven kind so its sides cannot be seen through.

A rectangular metal tray, approximately 9″ x 14″.

A tabloid size newspaper, or a newspaper magazine section.

Scotch tape, scissors, and a razor blade in a holder.

How you make the props:

The narrow edges of the material will be at the top and bottom of the bag. It is made by separately hemming the tops of the three pieces and then by sewing all three together with a French seam down the sides and across the bottom. The seams are turned to the inside. You now should have a bag divided inside into two sections by a piece of material in the middle.

With the razor blade in a holder, cut one of the table tennis balls in half at its seam. Take one of the halves and neatly trim off another $\frac{1}{16}''$ with the scissors. Discard the other half of the ball.

Roll a double sheet of the tabloid paper into a tube large enough in diameter for the balls to drop through it freely and easily. Fasten the tube with strips of tape near the top, center and bottom. Since you will have to make a paper tube each time you do the trick, you may find it easier to form a number of them at the same time by rolling the paper around a cardboard mailing tube of proper diameter. When packing the show, you can also use the cardboard tube to keep inside the paper tube and prevent its crushing in your suitcase.

How you use them:

With your left hand, pick up the bag by its left top corner and hold it in front of you. Put one of the balls into the rear part of the bag with your right hand. Now hold the bag between both hands by its top corners so that your two thumbs are in the front section. By keeping your hands that way and gathering the material up into your fingers, you can turn the bag inside out and the ball will seem to have disappeared.

You will find you can do the same thing with four of the balls in the rear section of the bag, because of their light weight and the natural friction of the material. Nothing will fall out and nothing will be heard if you handle the bag this way in a slow and deliberate manner and don't wave it in the air or try to hurry too much when turning it inside out. Do it smoothly and casually, not as though you were hiding anything, and try to forget the balls are there. With the bag inside out, you can show all sides of it. Gather it up into your fingers in the same way once more to turn it right side out again.

Now try something else. First empty the right pocket of your trousers. Then put one of the balls into the front section of the bag and another into the rear section. Take the ball out of the front of the bag, show it, and put it into your pocket. Turn the bag inside out to show it empty and then turn it right side out again. Gather the top of the bag together and hold it with your left hand. You are about to make the ball vanish from your pocket and appear in the bag.

Put your right hand into your pocket and push the ball that is there to the top of the pocket with your thumb as you pull the pocket lining inside out. The ball seems to have vanished from your pocket. Push the pocket lining back in, show your hand empty, and reach into the bag and take out the duplicate ball. It appears as if the ball flew from your pocket into the bag. Now you can make it go back from the bag into your pocket. Show the ball and put it into the rear section of the bag. Wave your hand over it and then gather up the material between your hands to turn the front section inside out and show the bag empty. Reach into your pocket and produce the ball, which magically seems to have gone back where it started.

The next props to try are the paper tube and the basket. Put the half-ball rim upwards in the basket and the other four balls with it. Hold the tube upright over the basket with your left hand. Your fingers should be around it near the bottom so you can put your little finger beneath the opening.

THE LITTLE BLACK BAG

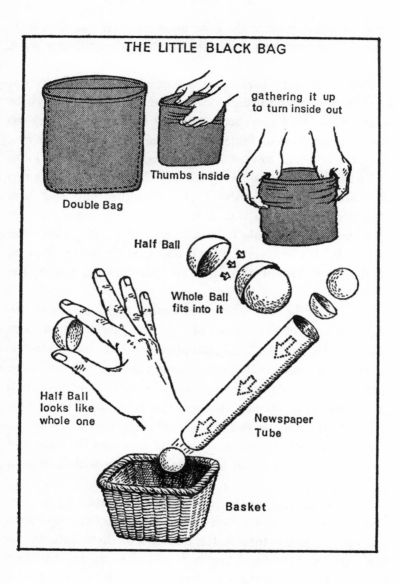

Double Bag

Thumbs inside

gathering it up
to turn inside out

Half Ball

Whole Ball
fits into it

Half Ball
looks like
whole one

Newspaper
Tube

Basket

Squeeze the bottom of the tube together a little so that balls dropped into it won't fall right on through until you want to release them.

With your right hand, pick up one of the balls, drop it into the top of the upright tube, and let it fall through to where your left fingers stop it at the bottom. Now pick up the half-ball so your fingers and thumb hold it by the rim. Turn the ball part toward the front and hold it up so it looks like a full ball. Tilt the top of the tube back slightly and drop the half-ball into the tube. Pick up another ball and drop that into the tube on top of it. As they fall down into the tube, one of the whole balls automatically will go into the half-ball. This happens by itself and is nothing you have to think about. Finally drop a third ball into the top of the tube.

Hold the tube well above the basket and let each of the balls drop out of the bottom of the tube, one at a time, and fall into the basket. You apparently put four balls into the tube, but because one has gone inside the half-ball only three seem to fall out. As far as the audience is concerned, one ball has vanished in passing through the tube. If you put two balls into the tube with the half-ball, only two will seem to drop out. Finally if you drop the half-ball into the tube and drop a whole ball in on top of it, only one will appear to drop out.

To set things up for the routine, put the basket to the left side of the tray, put the half-ball in the basket rim upwards, and rest the paper tube in the basket. Put three balls in the back section of the black bag and one ball in the front section and lay the bag on the tray next to the basket. Make sure your right pocket is empty.

What you say and do:

MAGICIAN: I'd like to show you one of the oldest tricks in magic.

(Left hand picks up black bag by left corner and displays it.)

It involves a little black bag ...

(Right hand reaches into front section, brings out ball, holds it up to show it, and drops ball to tray on table.)

... and a little white ball.

(Both hands hold bag between them, thumbs in front section, and fingers gather up material to turn bag inside out.)

This is one of the first tricks I ever saw a magician do. It's still one of my favorites.

(Shows both sides of bag and turns it right side out again.)

The idea is that you put the little ball into the bag ...

(Right hand picks up ball from tray, shows it and slowly and gently puts it into rear section. Hand withdraws, is casually shown empty, and drops to side. Left hand bunches top of bag together and holds bag high.)

... and cast a magic spell over it that makes the ball invisible.

(Wiggles right fingers to cast "spell" on bag. Both hands hold bag between them, thumbs in front section, and fingers gather up material and slowly turn bag inside out. Left hand shows both sides of bag.)

Naturally, the little ball is very hard to see when it's invisible.

(Hands turn bag right side out again. Left hand bunches top and holds bag high.)

But if you take away the magic ...

(Right hand waves at bag, which lets audience see hand is empty, and then reaches into rear of bag and slowly removes ball, holding it up to display it.)

... then the little ball becomes visible again ... Let's try it once more.

(Right hand replaces ball gently in rear section, but comes out closed, as if hand were concealing ball. Right hand moves swiftly to left armpit, as though tucking ball under arm to hide it there, and quickly comes away. Left upper arm stays pressed tightly to side, pretending to hide ball. While left fingers bunch top of bag, right hand is waved to cast "spell.")

A little magic to make it invisible ...

(Some of audience may shout ball is under his arm. Pays no attention, but goes right on with trick, whether there is shouting or not. Takes bag between hands, thumbs in front section, gathers material in fingers and turns bag inside out.)

... and it's gone once more.

(Turns bag right side out. Holds it in front of him and lifts both elbows high while displaying bag, also revealing in a subtle way, without making a deliberate gesture to show there is nothing under his arm, that ball isn't hidden there.)

It goes and it comes.

(Right hand reaches into rear section, takes ball from bag, shows it and drops ball to tray.)

A little white ball ... and a little black bag.

(Right hand picks up ball from tray and shows it. He turns side slightly so audience has clear view and puts ball into right pocket of trousers.)

This time, we'll make it fly through the air.

(Snaps right finger and thumb in front of pocket. Reaches into pocket with right hand. Thumbs ball to top of pocket and pulls out lining to show pocket empty. Pushes lining back in.

Withdraws hand and casually shows hand empty as he brings it above bag and snaps thumb and finger again.)

Did you see it go? Well, it did.

(*Right hand reaches into rear of bag and takes out ball, holds it up and shows it, replaces it gently in rear section.*)

We might as well use the other half of the round-trip ticket.

(*Snaps right fingers above bag, then quickly snaps them again in front of pocket. Reaches into pocket and produces ball, holds it up to show it.*)

It took the express ... no stops along the way.

(*This time, instead of replacing ball gently in bag, right hand throws it deliberately, with some force, into rear section. A loud click is heard as the ball strikes the others that have been concealed there. Left hand rattles bag a bit, but not obviously, to make sure sound is heard. Magician glances with apparent embarrassment at bag and then out at audience.*)

Some of you seem a bit suspicious. I heard what you just whispered to your friend, sir ...

(*Points toward someone in audience. Speaks as if first denying it, then smiles as he finishes speaking.*)

... you said I had more than one little white ball ... well, you were absolutely right!

(*Right hand reaches into bag and produces the balls, one at a time, dropping each to the tray.*)

I have one ... two ... three ... four!

(*Left hand drops bag on table to discard it. Right hand picks up balls one at a time from tray and drops them into basket.*)

One ... two ... three ... four.

(*Left hand picks up paper tube and holds it upright with fingers at bottom.*)

Seeing is not always believing. Will you please all count aloud with me as I drop these balls into the top of the tube?

(*Steps behind table. Reaches into basket with right hand, picks up one of balls, and drops it into top of tube as left hand tilts tube backwards slightly to receive it. Ball falls down inside until left fingers stop it at bottom.*)

One . . .

(*Looks out at audience and coaxes them to count aloud. Right hand reaches into basket, takes out half-ball by rim, holds it up to show it as if it were another ball, and drops that into top of tube tilted back to receive it.*)

. . . two . . .

(*Right hand picks up another ball and drops it into top of tube same way.*)

. . . three . . .

(*Right hand takes another and drops that into tube.*)

. . . four . . . Now will everybody count the balls with me again as they come out the bottom of the tube? Everybody, please . . . out loud.

(*Left hand slowly releases the balls, one at a time, as audience counts aloud with him.*)

One . . . two . . . three?

(*He counts the last one as if he were about to go on and say, "four," then looks up at audience questioningly when no more balls fall out the bottom of the tube. One seems to have disappeared.*)

Let's count them again.

(*As he makes the count, right hand takes one ball from basket and drops it into top of tube, then takes half-ball, shows it as full ball and drops that, then takes another ball and drops that into tube.*)

One . . . two . . . three. Count with me again as they come from the bottom of the tube.

(*Left hand releases them, one at a time, to drop from bottom of tube into basket.*)

One . . . two?

(*Pauses, looks out at audience, waits a second for vanish to register. Reaches into basket with right hand, picks up half-ball and drops that into tube, then picks up another ball and drops that in.*)

One . . . two in the top.

(*Left hand releases the ball and the covering half-ball that drop as one from the bottom of the tube to the basket.*)

One?

(*Pauses, looks out at audience, and then walks forward, holding upright tube in left hand, fingers squeezing it at the bottom slightly as if keeping the balls inside it.*)

I know what you're all thinking . . .

(*Glances at tube and then at audience.*)

. . . but really . . . it isn't so!

(*As he speaks, he crushes the tube between both hands, crumples it up and smiles. Holds it a moment and then throws empty wad of paper high into the air and out into audience as he bows to applause.*)

The Orange Swindle

YOU NOW have the audience warmed up so that they have joined in the fun, taking an indirect part in the show by counting aloud with you as the little balls dropped through the tube. Now you can lead some of them into "getting into the act" directly, by choosing volunteers to help you.

But when choosing them, don't make a general request for "a volunteer from the audience." If you do, you may have trouble coaxing someone to come up, which will mean a delay that can ruin the pace of your act, or else you may be stampeded by a rush of eager youngsters. Instead, watch your audience as you perform, and make up your mind ahead of time which persons you will choose to take part in the tricks that require it. Then go directly to one of those persons, put something into his hands, and ask him to help in some specific way. Don't ask, "I wonder if you will assist me in this next trick?" Hand him some object and say, for example, "Will you please open this paper bag? Just bring it over here to my table, sir, where everybody can see us."

Look for those who seem to be enjoying your show, those who laugh or applaud the most, but try to avoid the smart-

31

aleck type. Never, for any reason, ridicule or embarass anyone from the audience. Remember that he is a representative
of the entire group. If you make a fool of him, people may
laugh for a moment, but it will put you at odds with those
watching and in a position of challenging them to outwit you,
which will cause them to resist being fooled by your tricks
instead of enjoying the surprise of them. It is one thing to
lead the audience along by pretending to let people guess
how a trick may be done and then turning the whole thing
into general laughter, but quite another to cause anyone
genuine embarrassment.

For this routine, you should mentally choose a good-na-
tured man, not a child, who will be willing to let you borrow
a dollar bill. But at the start, you make no mention of that.
You show him a puzzle with a "magic orange" that you free
from two red ribbons he helps you to hold. When he agrees
that the orange is a remarkable one, you try to sell it to him
for a dollar. He naturally refuses to pay that much for an
orange, so you put it aside and tell him to forget it, that there
is another magical puzzle you would like to show him.

You borrow a dollar bill from him, have him write down
the serial number so it can be identified later, and then place
the dollar in an envelope, promising you will pay him back.
After asking him if he has ever seen a magician saw a woman
in half, you announce that you are about to saw George
Washington into halves. You cut through the envelope, and
apparently through the dollar bill, but instead of the paper
halves, two silver half-dollars drop from the envelope into
his hands. Having kept your promise to pay him back a dollar,
you ask him once again if he wouldn't like to invest it by buying your "magic orange." When he refuses, you tell him he
has passed up a good bargain and show him why. Cutting

open the orange, you find the original dollar bill, the one proven to be his by its serial number. If he had bought the "magic orange," he could have had two dollars. But you keep the bill and he keeps the two silver half-dollars and everything is square.

Removing the orange from the ribbons depends on a principle well-known to magicians as having first been used in a very old trick known as "Grandma's Necklace," in which three wooden beads were removed from a pair of strings. In this version, the ribbons are secretly doubled in half in a similar manner, and tied with thread around the middle so the doubled sections look like two continuous lengths.

The "sawed in half" dollar bill is exchanged for the two silver half-dollars by means of a tricked envelope and the dollar bill finally found in the orange is not really the borrowed one, but a duplicate put there beforehand. The serial number, which you read aloud to him at the time he copies it, is that of the duplicate bill.

What you need:

A cardboard or plastic box large enough to hold all the props for the trick and decorative in appearance.

Two red ribbons, each ½" wide and about 50" long.

A spool of matching red silk or cotton (not nylon) thread.

A tapestry or bookbinder's needle. This should be at least 3½" long and have a large eye.

A plate small enough to fit into the box with the other things.

A small paring knife.

Several paper napkins, to wipe your hands after handling the cut orange.

One medium-sized orange.

Half a dozen 3″ x 5″ index cards and a rubber band to go around them.

Two pencils. (The second one is to have on hand in case the point of the first should break while you are performing.)

A 6¾″ white envelope. This is the standard small business envelope. Any envelope of approximate size will do.

Two silver half-dollars.

A dollar bill.

A razor blade in a holder.

White all-purpose glue.

A rectangular metal tray, large enough to hold the box and the plate beside it.

How you make the props:

With a pencil, lightly copy down the serial number of the dollar bill on one of the file cards, put a blank file card on top of that one, and then put those two on top of the other cards. Put the rubber band around them near the top of the packet so you can tell at a glance which end is up and won't have to read the number upside down.

Carefully pry up the pip of the orange with the point of the knife. Remove the pip and put it aside. Push a pencil through the opening where the pip was and gently bore a hole into the orange with it, but don't push it out through the skin on the other side. Starting at one end, roll up the dollar bill. Make this roll as small and tight as you can. Push the tightly rolled dollar bill into the hole in the orange. Force it down gently until it is entirely hidden inside. With a touch of glue, fasten the pip back in place on the orange and let it dry.

Lay one red ribbon on top of the other so both ends match. Tie a short length of red thread around the center of the ribbons, knot it tightly twice, and cut off the remaining thread about ½″ from the knots. Take one end of the *top* ribbon in your left hand and the other end of the top ribbon in your right hand, bring those ends together, and hold them up high. The result should be a loop of ribbon which has another loop hanging from it by the thread that fastens them. But if you cover the place where they are joined with your right hand, it will look as if you are holding two continuous lengths of ribbon. Now thread one set of ends through the eye of the needle far enough so the needle won't slip off them.

With the razor blade in a holder, cut a *vertical 2″* slit *down* the face of the envelope, *but not through the back of it,* from a point at its center and about 1½″ from the top. You may find this easiest to do by slipping a piece of cardboard into the envelope to keep from cutting through its back. Probably you will want to make up a number of these envelopes to practice using them. With the back of the slitted envelope towards you, put the two half-dollars together in the bottom right corner of it.

How you use them:

You will have to learn to handle the ribbons so as not to reveal that they are joined by thread. Fix them by rolling the two ribbons together neatly around the top end of the needle until you come to the part where they are joined. This is the way they should be kept in the box of props. It lets you pick them up without fumbling. Just take the part where they join between your right thumb and first finger, pick them up, and the needle will unroll itself. With your left hand, take the needle and bring it up to your right hand. Your right thumb and first finger hold the needle along with the part of the ribbons they are already holding.

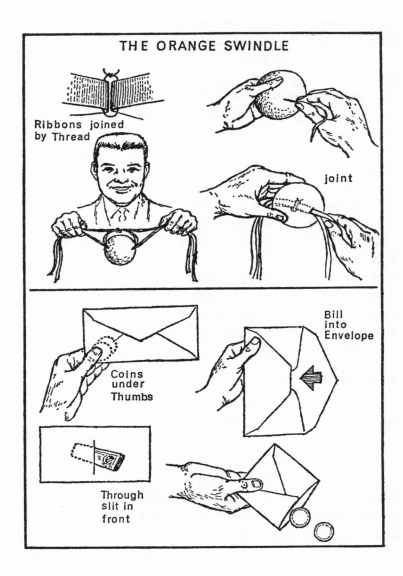

THE ORANGE SWINDLE

Ribbons joined by Thread

joint

Coins under Thumbs

Bill into Envelope

Through slit in front

With your left hand, pick up the orange. Push the needle into it and draw the ribbons through until the part where they are joined is hidden inside the orange. Remove the needle from the ribbons and discard it. Hold the orange and let all the ribbons drop. Take one ribbon from each side of the orange, cross them as if tying a knot, and draw them tight upon the orange.

At this point, if you were actually performing, you would have your helper from the audience take two ends of the ribbon while you take the other two. For practice, you can tie his two ends to the top of a chair back and pretend someone is holding them. Hold both your ends tightly with your left hand. Grasp the orange with your right hand, pull down sharply, and it will come free of the outstretched ribbons, seeming to pass right through them.

The business of making a fake record of the serial number of the dollar bill is done this way: After you have borrowed the bill, pick up the packet of file cards and a pencil. Pull the top card from under the rubber band that is around the packet and hand your helper that card and the pencil. Rest the dollar bill on the remaining cards in your hand. Pretend to read aloud the number on the bill as he copies it on his card, but really read the serial number of the duplicate bill already hidden in the orange, the number you penciled in advance on the card that is now the top one in your hand.

To try the trick envelope with the vertical slit, start by folding a dollar bill in half, then in quarters, and then once more. Hold it in your left hand. With your right hand, pick up the envelope at the corner where the half-dollars are concealed, pressing them between your thumb and finger. Holding the envelope flat with its back upwards, put the folded dollar on it, under your right thumb. Show it that way a moment. Then bring your open left hand up under the envelope, so the envelope rests on the palm of that hand. With your right hand, put the dollar bill into the envelope, but push it crosswise right on through the slit into your left hand.

Underneath the envelope, flatten your left fingers so they conceal the bill against it. Lift the envelope to your mouth with your left hand and lick the flap. Bring it down flat in front of you again and seal the envelope by pressing the flap with your right fingers. With your right finger and thumb, grip the corner where the coins are concealed. Turn your body a little to the left, reach into the prop box with your turned down left hand, drop the dollar bill, and bring out the scissors.

Transfer the scissors to your right hand and take the envelope with your left, gripping it at the corner where the coins are hidden. Cut the envelope in half with the scissors, feeling beneath it as you do so as to cut right along the slit. Give the empty half of the envelope to your helper. Then have him cup his hands so you can dump the half-dollars into them from the other half of the envelope and then give him that piece of the envelope.

Finding the other dollar in the orange at the end of the trick requires only cutting the orange open to reveal it.

To set things up, put the orange with its hidden bill into the prop box next to the needle around which you have rolled the prepared ribbons in the way explained so that you can pick them up without fumbling. Place the envelope with its half-dollars in that side of the box in a position so that you can pick it up correctly. Put the file cards, pencils, paring knife, scissors and paper napkins into the box. Have the small plate beside the box on the tray. For packing, the box should have a lid so everything can be carried in it ready to use, but it is left uncovered while performing.

What you say and do:

MAGICIAN: I have a friend who grows the most remarkable oranges in his cellar.

(*Takes orange from box, shows it, and goes to person he has decided will be his helper from the audience.*)

Have a look at this one, sir. (*Puts orange in helper's hand.*) You'd hardly think my friend could grow that in his cellar, would you? Of course . . . he's a magician, too. Would you bring the orange right up here, please?

(*Leads helper to come up and stand at his right near table.*)

When magicians get together, they sometimes have fun making up magical puzzles for each other to solve. Here's one my orange-growing magician friend asked me to solve when I had dinner at his house the other night. He said . . . suppose you take an orange . . .

(*Takes orange from helper. Tosses it from right hand to left and holds it up.*)

. . . and then you take two ribbons . . .

(*Right hand takes ribbons from box, concealing where they are joined, and lets needle fall down.*)

. . . and thread the ribbons right through the center of the orange.

(*Does so, removing needle and discarding it on tray. Holds up orange with ribbons hanging.*)

And then suppose you tie the orange firmly in place at the center.

(*Ties ribbons over orange and then hands helper two ends of the ribbons.*)

Hold these tightly, will you, sir? One in each hand.

(*Holds his own ends of ribbons in left hand.*)

Now, my friend said ... here's the puzzle ... how would you remove the orange from the ribbons without breaking the ribbons or cutting the orange in half? Well, I thought it over a minute and said ... I think I'd cut an invisible hole in the orange right about here.

(*With right fingertip, he touches orange, pointing to where he would cut imaginary hole.*)

Then I'd pull the ribbons right through the invisible hole.

(*With right hand, suddenly pulls orange free of ribbons. Holds ribbons and orange as they are a moment. Looks out at audience and smiles.*)

My friend agreed that was exactly how he would do it, too.

(*Takes applause. After pause, takes ribbons from helper and discards them in box. Holds up orange to him.*)

That's quite an orange, isn't it, sir? How would you like to own a magic orange? I'll sell you this one ... for a dollar. No? All right, we'll forget the orange.

(*Puts it on plate, still in full view.*)

How about letting me borrow a dollar then? While you're here, I'd like to show you another magical puzzle. Will you lend me a dollar ... for just a few minutes? I promise to pay you back.

(*Holds out his hand for it. When helper gives him dollar, he looks down at bill, then at helper, and smiles.*)

You do trust me, don't you? Maybe you'd feel better if we had a record of this financial transaction.

(*Takes file cards and pencil from box. Gives helper top card and pencil.*)

Will you copy down the serial numbers of your dollar, please?

(Holds bill on packet of cards in hands. Slowly and clearly reads aloud numbers penciled secretly on card that now is atop packet in hand. As he reads, helper copies them.)

Just put that into your pocket where you can find it later ... in case something should happen to this dollar.

(Takes back pencil, discards it in box with file cards.)

You've heard of a magician sawing a woman in halves?

(Folds bill and holds it up with left hand. With right hand, reaches into box, picks up envelope at corner where half-dollars are. Presses them and brings envelope out, back upwards and flat before him. Rests dollar bill under thumb on envelope. Brings left hand up under envelope. Pushes dollar bill into envelope and secretly right on out through slit into left hand. Seals envelope.)

Well, you're about to see George Washington sawed into halves.

(Turns slightly to left. With left hand reaches into box, dropping dollar bill and bringing out scissors, which he snips in air.)

You don't mind if I cut right through your dollar, do you?

(Transfers scissors to right hand. Grips coin corner of envelope with left. Holding envelope flat before him, he cuts through its center with scissors, feeling underneath to cut along line of slit. Hands helper half of envelope that is empty.)

Will you see if one half is in there? ... No? Well, both halves must be in this end then. Will you hold out your hands, sir? Just cup them together so you can catch the pieces.

(Dumps half-dollars out of envelope into helper's hands.)

There you are ... the two halves!

(Gives helper other half of envelope to look over if he wishes and discards scissors.)

You now have your money back, just as I promised.

(*Picks up orange from plate.*)

Are you sure you wouldn't like to change your mind and invest that dollar in this magic orange? I'll still sell it. The price hasn't gone up. One dollar for an orange ... No? Well that's an offer you should have taken. I told you it was a real bargain. I'll show you why.

(*Takes knife from box. Puts orange on plate. Cuts orange through center. Holds half of orange in front of him so audience can see and slowly plucks out dollar bill. Discards orange half on plate.*)

Remember the record you made of our transaction? You have it in your pocket. The serial numbers of your dollar bill.

(*Unrolls bill slowly. Holds it outstretched between hands.*)

Check these numbers as I read them.

(*Steps beside helper and holds bill so helper can see it and compare with numbers on card as he dramatically reads them aloud.*)

It checks exactly, sir? ... If you'd bought the orange, you could have had this dollar, too. But since you have the two halves, I'll keep this soggy dollar bill and we'll call it square ... Thank you.

(*Wipes hand dry with paper napkin, shakes helper's hand. Turns to audience and smilingly leads applause for helper as man returns to his seat. Bows to applause, and then completes wiping hands and discards napkin.*)

The Magic Tax

WHEN THE famous American magician, Milbourne Christopher, brought his show, *Christopher's Wonders*, to Broadway several years ago, audiences loved one of the small gems of magic that stood out among all the other clever and elaborate illusions he presented. It was the ancient trick of seeming to catch coins from the air, but Christopher dressed it up with a new theme that made it freshly appealing. Most people wish they could pluck money from the air and many also wish they had some magic way to pay their taxes. He played on both those wishes by being a magical tax collector. Although the trick was only a brief interlude in his big show, the tax collecting theme made a decided hit.

It also will make a fine ending for your club show. The tax collecting idea is amusing, the presentation quick and direct, and the clinking sound of the money adds greatly to the appeal. While the method Christopher used in his show was, of course, not the same as that revealed here, he has been kind enough to give the author permission to borrow the theme around which to build a story you can use in your own show.

The secret depends on an illusion of sound. You seem to catch coins from the air at your fingertips and drop them, one by one, into a cardboard bucket. Actually, you have only one coin in your hand, which is tricked in a simple manner so you can make it appear or vanish at will. In the bucket, there is a hidden cardboard half-shelf, upon which the other coins flatly rest. You brush them off the shelf, one at a time, so they fall loudly to the bottom of the bucket as you pretend to deposit the coins you are catching. Because of its construction, it is possible to handle the bucket so as to go on producing coins for as long as you wish. However, since the effect is one that can become boring instead of amusing if it is carried on too long, this routine has been kept brief. It should be performed in a brisk and fast-paced manner.

What you need:

Eleven half-dollars or weighty play money coins the same approximate size.

Two cardboard paint tubs. These look like giant cardboard drinking cups, are about 6″ tall, 8″ in diameter at the top and 6″ in diameter at the bottom, and may be purchased in most paint or hardware stores.

A strong pair of scissors.

A roll of white or clear plastic adhesive tape.

A rectangular metal tray, about 9″ x 14″ in size.

How you make the props:

With the scissors, cut away and discard all of one of the cardboard tubs except for the bottom and as much of the tub as extends up for about 1½″ above the bottom on all sides. Now cut away a 2″ section of this piece on a straight line, down one side, across the bottom, and up the other side.

Discard the part cut off. What you should have left is about three-quarters of the bottom, with a narrow collar of cardboard extending up around the back of it. This becomes the hidden shelf upon which the coins will rest.

Put it inside the tub that is still whole, about halfway down and against one of the sides and fix it there by taping the cardboard collar to the side of the tub. Fasten it as firmly as possible. The shelf should be tilted very slightly toward the side to which it is attached so the coins won't slide off it prematurely.

To make the trick coin that you will produce from your hand, take one of the coins and fasten one end of a 2¼″ strip of the clear plastic tape to the center of it, so the rest of the strip extends out flatly to the side.

How you use them:

Try the coin first. Put it on a table with the strip of tape to the right and its sticky side up. Stand in front of it and bring your right hand down so the middle joint of your first finger is at the edge of the coin and on the tape. Press your palm flat, lift your hand, and then relax your fingers completely. The tape should stick to the inside surfaces of your first two fingers so the coin hangs there and is hidden when the back of your hand is toward the audience. Give the tape a squeeze with your thumb to make it stick tightly.

Now gently swing your hand upward and forward a little. The coin will hinge on the tape and flop itself up to the top edge of your index finger. Put the tip of your thumb against the bottom edge of the coin to hold it there. Holding it that way, wiggle the coin back and forth a little so it will reflect the light and can be seen better. If you turn your hand down as if you were dropping the coin and just let go of it entirely it will hang again by its tape and be hidden by your fingers. You can forget it's there and just hold your hand as you naturally would.

Turn your body to the left. Bring your right hand up and reach into the air. Give your hand a little upward and forward jerk and the coin will appear. Hold your left hand palm upwards. Turn your right hand over as if you were putting the coin into your left hand. Close your left fingers and drop your right hand to your side. Slowly open your left hand and show that the coin has vanished. Reach into the air with your right hand and produce it again.

If you will try using this coin before your mirror, you will see what an excellent effect it has. Fool around with it, try various things with it, and practice using it until it really looks as if you were producing coins from the air. You can also pretend to take them from behind your knee, your other elbow, the heel of your shoe. Each time you perform, be sure to attach a fresh strip of tape to the coin because it doesn't stay sticky very long.

To try the bucket, lay ten coins flat on the hidden half-shelf. Put the bucket on a table so the shelf side is toward the front. Attach the taped coin to your right hand as usual. Reach up into the air with your hand and produce the coin. Show it and wiggle it in the light. Now just put your right hand down into the bucket as if you were dropping the coin. With your first finger, brush one of the coins off the shelf so it drops to the bottom of the tub. Remove your hand, reach into the air, and produce the coin again. Put your hand into the bucket and slide another coin off the shelf.

When all the coins are off the shelf, pick up the bucket with your right hand. Hold out your cupped left hand and dump the coins into it from the bucket. With your right

THE MAGIC TAX

Bucket
from
above

strip of
Tape on
Coin

Bucket

rear view

front view

pushing
coins
off shelf
into Bucket

Paying
through
the nose

hand, turn the bucket upright again. Hold your left hand above it and spill the coins down into the bucket so they strike the hidden shelf and land there. Some may fall to the bottom, but most will stay on the shelf. Now you can go right on producing coins again and brushing them off the shelf inside the bucket as before.

The bucket doesn't have to be on the table while you are catching coins. You can walk around with it, holding it high and tilted slightly with your left hand at the top while your right hand works the taped coin, pretending to pull coins from the pockets, hair or clothing of members of the audience. You do it the same way, but you must remember to keep the bucket high enough so nobody can look into it. Just hold it by the top at the back, with your left fingers inside and your thumb outside.

When you have finished catching coins, dump them all out into your cupped right hand. Rest the bucket on the table and hold your hand high above it. Let most of the coins spill down into the bucket, but hold some back, so they are hidden in your right hand. Drop your right hand to your side a moment. Then bring your hand up to your nose, open your fingers and let the coins fall from the bottom of them into the bucket. It will look as though you produced a shower of them from your nose.

To set things up, put the bucket on the tray, turn it so the side with the shelf is toward the front, and lay ten coins flat on the shelf. Lay the other coin, with a new strip of tape attached, on the tray behind the bucket, with the strip to the right and its sticky side up.

What you say and do:

MAGICIAN: I'm very sorry to have to interrupt the performance at this time. But before I say good night, I have to
collect the magic tax.

(*Stands behind table. With left hand, moves bucket forward a little on tray. Secretly presses right hand on tape so
coin sticks to fingers and, as part of same motion, brings right
hand up to touch side of bucket as though straightening it.
Drops right hand to side.*)

It's the new state law, you know . . . so I hope you'll pardon
me for a minute while I become a tax collector.

(*Turns right side to audience. Looks into air in front of
him as if he sees something there.*)

There's one now.

(*With right hand, reaches into air, produces coin and
pretends to drop it into bucket, really letting it fall behind
fingers as he brushes one from hidden shelf.*)

And another . . . and one more.

(*Produces them and pretends to drop into bucket in same
way.*)

The tax bureau will be pleased . . . collections are going
well tonight.

(*Produces several more as he speaks.*)

Don't you wish you could really pay your taxes this easily?
Just reach into the air . . . and there you are? . . . So do I.

(*Reaches for one, but finds nothing in his fingers. Smiles,
reaches down to heel of right shoe, lifting heel to his fingers
so he can produce coin.*)

That one nearly got away.

(*Picks up bucket with left hand, fingers inside top, thumb
at rear. With right hand plucks coin from left elbow.*)

Sometimes they stick up my sleeve.

(*Pretends to pull one from right ear.*)

They say that money talks ... it's no wonder I've been hard of hearing lately.

(*Puts bucket on table. Steps in front of table. With right hand, reaches up and produces coin.*)

Easy come ...

(*Holds out left hand. Pretends to put coin in it. Drops right hand naturally to side as he moves left hand up and away. Rubs left fingers together as if pulverizing coin and slowly opens them to show it gone.*)

... and easy go.

(*Reaches into air, produces it, pretends to drop in bucket.*)

But it didn't get far ... I wonder how much we have?

(*Dumps coins from bucket into cupped left hand. Lets them cascade from left hand to land on hidden shelf in bucket.*)

Not enough yet ... I don't think the tax bureau will be satisfied.

(*Takes bucket in left hand. Looks out at audience.*)

You don't mind if I collect a few from you, do you?

(*Holding bucket high and slightly tilted, hurries to front row of audience.*)

Here's one here ...

(*Pretends to pluck coin from spectator's hair, shows it and drops it in bucket.*)

... and you have one, sir ...

(*Pretends to take it from another man's breast pocket.*)

... right here in your pocket ...

(*Approaches woman holding gloves or some other article in her lap and pretends to take coin from her.*)

... and one over here in the glove the lady has been holding.

(*Looks at audience, shakes head, and smiles.*)

I'm afraid some of you have been claiming too many deductions ... no use holding out on the tax collector, you know. I'll get the money anyhow.

(*Catches another and pretends to drop it in bucket. Rattling bucket loudly, he hurries back to table. Dumps coins into right hand and lets them cascade into bucket, secretly holding back a few. Drops right hand naturally to side as he rattles bucket again with left hand. Holds bucket in front of him.*)

This is called ... paying through the nose.

(*Puts right hand to nose and lets coins fall from bottom of hand into bucket.*)

You've been a swell audience. This has been fun for me tonight and I hope it has been for you.

(*Rattles bucket and then slaps it with his right hand.*)

Thank you all for your taxes ... I'll take this over to town hall on my way home.

(*Puts bucket down. Lifts hands to encourage applause. Bows to it.*)

The Club Show Set-up

IF THE room where you are going to perform is one you are not familiar with, visit it well in advance of the show. Find out where you will be expected to set up your things, where the audience will be seated, whether there is a portable screen you may use, and if there are two tables and a chair available.

For this act, you will need two card tables, or tables of somewhat similar size, and a straight-backed chair. If you want to dress it up, you can have loose black slipcovers made in a size to fit average card tables and carry those with you, along with a matching slipcover for the back of the chair. You may prefer to carry your own tables. Suggestions for making simple magic tables are included in the next section of this book, which deals with a stage show. But they are not necessary for a club show of this kind.

One card table will be behind you. It is used to hold all the props for your act. Except for the first routine, *Under Your Spell*, which uses just the tube you hold in your hands, everything you need for each routine should be set on a separate tray. The trays should be lined up in the exact order in which you will perform the routines. Everything on each tray must be ready to use and in proper position so there will be no fumbling or delay.

To the left of that prop table, right next to it, you will have the chair, with its back to the audience. Your suitcase, with its lid open, will go on the chair. The second table is your working table. It is kept clear at all times except for the things that are part of the one routine you are performing. The working table should be several feet in front of the prop table and slightly to the right of it.

When you finish a routine, put everything that belongs to it back on the tray. As you pick up the tray from your working table, start the talk for your next routine, step back to the chair, and quickly put the things you have used into the suitcase, tray and all. Immediately pick up the next tray, put that on your working table, and continue the performance.

The routines should flow smoothly from one to the next, with no delays between. Don't take time to straighten things as you put them back into your suitcase. You can do that after the show or when you get home. Just put them there and go into what comes next. This does not mean, of course, that you should rush through the show itself. It should be done deliberately, with proper timing and pace, by acting out the magical stories, and never forgetting the part of the magician that your tricks are designed to help you play. When you finish a routine, take time, too, to acknowledge your applause. But then, once it definitely is over, move swiftly to the next thing.

Everything should be in your suitcase and both tables should be bare when you have finished your show. As you put the last props into it, shut down the lid. There will be nothing for anyone to handle or for inquisitive eyes to see.

You will be completely free to mingle with the guests or simply to pick up your suitcase and go home.

To prepare for the show at home, before you start to put anything into your suitcase, set everything out on a table in exactly the way it would be on your prop table during a performance. Make out a written card for each trick or routine, with the name of it at the top, a list of every prop needed, and then how it should be set up. Check the arrangement of the props for each routine against the card. Don't ever rely on memory. If you do, the time is almost sure to come when you will be embarrassed before an audience by having forgotten some tiny prop vital to your show.

Set up as many things as you can at home so they can be put into your suitcase ready to position on your prop table when you get to where you will give the show. In this show, everything but the coins in the bucket for *The Magic Tax* can be set up in advance, ready to perform. You will find plastic bags and newspaper, plus plenty of rubber bands, handy for packing things, but if you are going to use the routines frequently you should have special cloth bags made to hold everything for each of them.

Load the tube for *Under Your Spell* and put it in a plastic bag. Fix the set-up of the handkerchiefs and folder on the tray for *Fast and Slow,* wrap newspaper around the tray and fasten that with rubber bands. Put the balls in place in *The Little Black Bag* and put the bag in the bottom of its basket, then slip a cardboard mailing tube inside the paper tube that goes with it. Nest that tray under the one used for *Fast and Slow.* Make sure everything is set in the prop box for *The Orange Swindle* and put the lid on it. Put that tray under the others. Fix the special coin for *The Magic Tax* by sticking its tape lightly around the coin itself. Drop that coin and the rest of the coins into a plastic bag and put them into the cardboard bucket.

Now it is time to pack everything into the suitcase. When you get to where you're giving the show, unwrap each set of props, putting them on the table in order and position for the act, but leave *The Magic Tax* in the suitcase until last. Set that up inside the suitcase, so nobody out front can see what you're doing. Quietly lay the coins flat on their half-shelf, put the bucket on its tray, pull loose the sticky tape on the trick coin, place that behind the bucket and you're set. Put the tray in its place on the prop table with the others and in less than five minutes you've gotten the whole show ready to give.

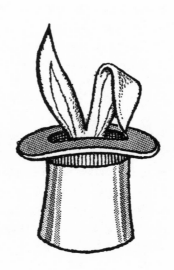

ACT TWO

On Stage

THIS IS the kind of a show you would give on a small stage, such as in a school or church auditorium, at a camp or community recreation center, wherever there is a platform that puts you apart from the audience and curtains to hide things from view while you set up your props. You can't very well leave the stage and go down into the audience to pass things around as you might during a club show. On the stage, you must hold the full attention of the audience at all times.

Audiences conditioned to smoothly professional TV entertainment expect a fast-moving show. For this reason, it is also wise to avoid tricks in which you need to call on people from the audience to assist you. If such effects are used at all, they should be used very sparingly because they interrupt the smooth pace that it is so necessary to maintain.

For this show, you will use a center working table, two side tables, a background screen, and a prop table that is behind the screen. The center table should be small, sturdy and uncovered, and about 33″ high. The top should be about

14" x 20". You can, of course, use an ordinary card table, or a wooden one borrowed wherever you perform. But it may be a little low for easy working and won't dress up the show as well as a magician's table of your own.

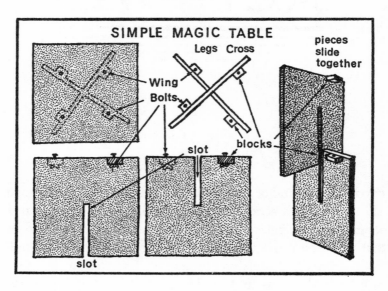

If you want to make one, a simple table can be constructed with pieces of ¼" plywood. The base is formed of two pieces, each 32" high by 18" wide. One should have a vertical slot ⅜" wide cut down from the center of the top for 16" to its middle. The other piece should have a slot of similar width and length running up from the bottom. These two become crosspieces. The one with the slot at the bottom is slid down across the one with the matching slot in the top, so they fit together and form legs that are at right angles.

The top, made of a 14" x 20" piece of ¼" plywood, may be covered with black velveteen or black plastic cloth. This is glued to the surface and tacked around the edges which are then covered with gold braid tape. If you prefer, the top may be sanded and enameled black, as the rest of the table should be. Four wing bolts, set into the top so they are flush with the surface, go through holes drilled in four matching blocks of ⅜″ wood screwed to the upper part of the base sections to hold the top in place. Such a table will knock down easily for packing. You should have a large canvas bag, with a drawstring top, to carry it in.

If you wish, two more of these may be used as your side tables, but TV snack tray tables or any fold-up tables of that approximate size will serve. To dress these up, you can paint their trays Chinese Red. You can use any available long table for your prop table, since it won't be seen. If you prefer to carry your own prop table, one of the folding metal ones, the kind that are about 50″ long and fold in half to be carried like a suitcase, will do well.

A background screen stands in front of the prop table. Again, you can construct your own frame for it, with two footed uprights and a cross bar at the top, all fastened with wing bolts and the parts hinged for easy packing into a carrying bag. But since there is hardly any school or church building where you will have difficulty in borrowing an ordinary three-panel folding screen, or the flat type on rollers, it is easier to use that to hang a cloth drape over.

The cloth can hang in draped folds, which will eliminate the problem of trying to make one to fit various types of screens. Use any plain black cloth of strong texture and sew it into a hemmed sheet that is about two yards square. You will also need some large metal clamp-type clips to fasten it. Hang the drape over the top of the screen so there is a good edge of material at the back. At each top corner, pull the top and side material together behind the screen and attach clamps. Six S-shaped picture hooks should be spaced along the top of the screen so you can hang Japanese lanterns from them.

Your working table is stage center, just back of the curtain line. Out to the left and right, and on a line slightly back of the working table, are the two side tables. The draped screen is at the back center, concealing the prop table directly behind it. There should be enough clearance so you can pass between the prop table and the back of the stage.

Hawaiian Magic

You open your show with something a little unexpected from the magician by using colorful Hawaiian *leis* as your unusual props for a series of quick surprises. Part of the routine is performed swiftly, in pantomime, after the brief spoken introduction.

As you tell how the Islanders give the traditional flower garlands to departing visitors in the hope that they may return some day, you put one of the *leis* around your neck, break it in two to symbolize the parting of friends, and restore it once more. You pass it through a tube and it changes color and then, from an empty box with an open window in its face, you produce a chain of garlands.

The secret of the broken *lei* is an extra loop, which is fixed to look like part of it and which you tear instead of the *lei* itself. Having it around your neck helps to hide the secret loop. You use the tube you made for *Under Your Spell* to change the color of the *lei*. The window box from which you produce the chain of garlands has a hidden compartment in which they are concealed.

What you need:

You use the imitation *leis* made of colored crepe paper which are available in many variety stores and at others where party goods are sold. For this routine, you will need three red, two green and one white, or the same number in substitute colors.

A spool of red cotton thread.

The color-changing tube made for *Under Your Spell.*

An empty cardboard facial tissue carton, about 5″ x 10″ in size, with an oval opening in the front that is about 7″ across, or any carton of similar size in which you cut an opening.

A sheet of white poster board.

A roll of ¾″ cloth adhesive tape.

Adhesive-backed decorative paper in two different patterns, one a design with a black background to stick to the inside surfaces of the box and the other to decorate the outside of it.

A magic wand, which you can make by painting a 12″ length of ½″ wooden dowel rod black and then giving it white tips in the traditional design by fastening strips of white plastic tape around the ends.

Scotch tape, a razor blade in a holder, a pencil, and white all-purpose glue.

One tray.

How you make the props:

Put the empty tissue carton, with its opening upwards, on the piece of poster board and trace around it with pencil. Cut the poster board just inside the pencil lines, so you have a piece slightly smaller than the bottom of the carton. Attach horizontal strips of cloth adhesive tape to the top and bottom edges of the piece of poster board so the tape extends about half its own width over those edges. Fold the tapes inward so the sticky half is up.

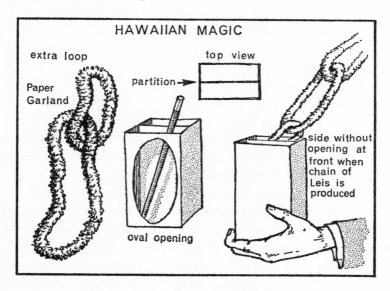

HAWAIIAN MAGIC

extra loop

Paper Garland

partition →

top view

oval opening

side without opening at front when chain of Leis is produced

Open both ends of the carton by carefully peeling loose the end tabs. Slide the piece of poster board into the carton so it is in the center of it and divides the carton in two sections. Press the attached strips of tape firmly to fix the partition in position there. Now glue the tabs at one end of the carton back into place, leaving the tabs at the other end open. You may want to reinforce these with extra pieces of poster board. The next step is to decorate the carton. With the black background adhesive-backed paper, cover the inside front section and its poster board partition. Decorate the outside with the other adhesive-backed paper.

To make the props for the other part of the routine, break off a 10″ length of one of the red paper *leis*, loop it around another red *lei,* and bind together the ends of the shorter piece by winding red thread around them. Now break the white one apart, thread one end of it through a red one and also a green one, and fasten the ends of the white one back together with Scotch tape.

How you use them:

The tube made for *Under Your Spell* is used much in the same way it was for that trick, but there is a slight difference in the handling of it. Because of the size of the garlands and the fact that they don't compress as readily as silk handkerchiefs, one garland has to be gradually pulled out of the tube as the other one is fed into it.

Start with a green garland hidden in the tube. Show the tube empty by opening it out between your hands as you did for *Under Your Spell.* Then hold the tube horizontally in your left hand, instead of vertically as in *Under Your Spell.* Push part of the red garland into the right end of the tube and pull a little of the green one out of the left end, then push in more of the red and pull out more of the green, and so on. The effect is that the garland changes color as it passes through. Finally hold up the green one and then turn the tube upright and once more show it empty by opening it out between your hands.

The *lei* that is broken and then restored is handled this way: Hold it with your right hand around where the small loop joins it. The small loop should be open above your hand. Show it that way. Then, still with your right hand, bring the *lei* straight up to your face and put it over your head so the extra loop goes well down on your shoulders back of your neck. Drop both hands to your sides a moment.

With your left hand, reach back behind your neck and grasp the bottom of the little loop, where it joins the big one. Slide the *lei* slowly around on your neck by bringing your left hand forward until you are holding the loop beneath your chin. While your left hand still holds it that way, bring up your right hand and separate the sides of the loop to show it clearly. Break the little loop in half and display the ends. Tear pieces from it and toss them away until the little loop is gone. Blow on the garland, spread it out between your hands to show it whole again, and then remove it from your neck.

To try the production box, put the chain of three *leis* in the secret rear compartment, turn the box so the open flaps are at the top, and rest the wand end-down in the front window compartment. Pick up the box with your left hand. Take the other end of the wand with your right hand, lift it a little, and then push that hand and the wand right out through the window of the box. Wave the wand. Pull your right hand out of the box and tap the wand in through the front of the window to show the box empty.

Put the wand under your left arm to hold it there. Turn your left hand so the back of the box is toward the audience. With your right hand, take the wand and wave it over the top of the box. Reach in and slowly pull out the garland chain.

Set things up for the routine by putting the red *lei* with the extra loop around it on the tray on your table. Load the green one into the hidden part of the tube, put a rubber band around the tube, and put it on the tray. Load the production box with the chain of garlands and also put that on the tray. Rest the wand end-down in the box.

What you say and do:

MAGICIAN: (*Enters briskly as curtains open, comes to front center of stage, and bows.*)

Aloha . . .

(*Holds up red garland.*)

. . . here's magic from Hawaii.

(*Right hand puts garland over head.*)

It's a pleasant custom in Hawaii to give a garland of flowers to a departing friend.

(*Right hand drops naturally to side. Left hand pulls garland around neck to show it, holds bottom of loop under chin. Right hand comes up and widens loop.*)

For a time, friendships may be broken.

(*Right hand breaks loop, shows ends, tears pieces from them and throws them away until loop is gone.*)

But the Islanders say that when the warm winds blow . . .

(*Blows breath on garland.*)

. . . travelers will return . . .

(*Spreads garland between thumbs to show it whole.*)

. . . and good friends will be together once more.

(*Leaves garland around neck. Picks up tube and shows it empty. With left hand, holds tube sidewise. Right hand takes garland from neck and pushes it part way into tube. Transfers tube to right hand. Pulls a little of green garland from other end of tube. Continues pushing in red and pulling out green until all of green can be shown. Holds it up, then drops it to tray on table. Shows tube empty and drops that beside it. Shows box empty by waving wand through it as practiced and then produces chain of three garlands. All of this, silently and swiftly. Places everything on tray, steps back and leaves tray on prop table behind screen, and immediately comes forward with props for next trick.*)

No Soap

A QUICK comedy routine now, in which you pretend to reveal the secret of a trick by giving the audience a backstage view, but finish leaving your spectators more puzzled
than ever. This is partly a build-up for the next routine to
come, in which they are sure they have caught on, until all
sorts of strange things happen. It also is an amusing little
interlude in itself.

You show what you say was part of a TV commercial. On
a small tray which has a concealing drape at the front, there
is a bar of soap and a metal tube. You tap the soap to prove
it solid, put it in the tube, and it vanishes. Then you offer
to explain how it is done by giving the audience a chance
to see how it would look if they were all seated backstage.
You turn the tray around so they can see that the front drape
hides a hole in the tray and a net beneath it so that the
soap drops through the hole into the net. But when you perform it for them once again, you pull the drape away to
reveal that the soap hasn't gone into the net after all. The
net, as well as the tube, is empty and the soap has vanished.

Its secret depends on the use of a paper soap wrapper,

fixed to look like a solid bar of soap, and weighted at one end so it sounds solid when you tap it on the tray. But in putting it into the tube the last time, you secretly crush it and hide it in your hand so it seems to have disappeared.

What you need:

A wide-mesh black net, the sort women put over their hair to keep curlers in place, or any other net with a mesh wide enough to be seen through from a distance.

A bar of soap with a paper or foil wrapper around it.

A 9" x 14" piece of heavy cardboard, such as the end flap of a cardboard box used for holding cans of soup. This is to be used as a tray so it must be strong enough to hold the weight of things you put on it. You may prefer to make the tray of ¼" plywood.

If cardboard is used, you will need a sheet of black adhesive-backed decorative paper.

A spool of strong buttonhole thread and a needle, plus a large nail to poke holes through the cardboard for attaching the net, or a drill to make such holes if plywood is used for the tray.

A lead weight, the kind fishermen use on their lines, large enough to make a good sound when tapped through paper against the tray.

Black elastic cord.

A quart size fruit juice can with top and bottom cleanly removed and the label taken off.

Black cloth or plastic ¾" adhesive tape.

An 18" square of heavy black cloth.

White all-purpose glue.

A razor blade in a holder, or a saw to cut a square opening in plywood.

How you make the props:

Cut a 3″ square opening about 2″ from the right side and 2″ from the front of the cardboard or plywood. Punch or drill a series of small holes around this for fastening the net. Sew the net in place beneath the opening with needle and thread. The bottom of the net should hang down about 4″ under the opening in the tray. Punch or drill a hole near each side of the tray, about ½″ in from the front edge.

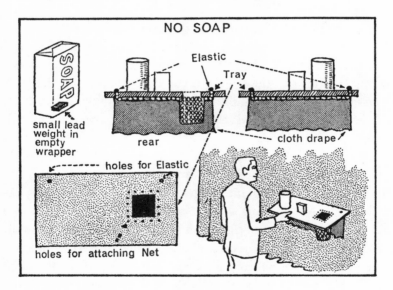

If you are using plywood, paint the tray black. If cardboard is used, cover it with the adhesive-backed black paper. Trim the edges of the tray with bands of the black adhesive tape and also use that to trim the opening and to cover the holes around it where the net has been stitched. Thread black elastic cord through one of the holes at the front of the tray and tie it tightly. Run the other end of the cord elastic through the hole at the other side. Tie it off there so the elastic runs along the front of the tray from one side to the other.

Carefully peel open one end of the soap wrapper without tearing it. Slide out the bar of soap and discard it. Drop the fishing weight inside the wrapper. Then seal the end of the wrapper back together with glue. You may want to make a quantity of these fake bars of soap for practicing the routine.

How you use them:

Put the cloth over the elastic that runs along the front edge of the tray. Pull it down in back until it is firmly held by the elastic. This should form a skirt or drape that hangs down along the front of the tray. Put the tube made from the fruit can at the left side of the tray and stand the fake bar of soap on end beside it. The little lead weight in the bottom will help keep it upright.

With your left hand, hold the tray in front of you by its left corner so the drape is toward the audience. Lift up the tube with your right hand, fingers well inside and thumb outside, and hold it up to show it empty. Rest the tube on the tray again. With your right hand, pick up the soap, show it, and tap the weighted bottom of it on the tray so it makes a sound. Put it (don't drop it) inside the tube. Move the tube to the right until the soap falls through the opening into the net, and then move the tube back where it was. With the right fingers inside the top of the tube and thumb outside, lift the tube and show that it is empty and the soap has vanished.

Now you are going to pretend to give the audience a back-stage view that exposes how it was done. Turn so you are facing left and the back edge of the tray is toward the audience. Hold it well away from your body so spectators will have a clear view. Then repeat the same moves: Show the tube empty, holding it the same way, tap the soap on the tray, put it into the tube, move it over the opening and let it drop into the net, move the tube back and show it empty. All of this is performed as if the audience were seated at the back of the stage.

Face front once more and seem to repeat the trick, but with a difference the audience shouldn't notice. Take the soap out of the net and tap it on the tray. With your right fingers inside the top of the tube and thumb outside as before, hold up the tube, show it empty, and rest it on the tray. Put the soap inside the tube with your right hand, but as you do, crush the wrapper into a tight wad in your hand. Move your hand on down to the bottom of the tube. Then bring your hand to the top until you can move your thumb outside. Squeeze your fingers against the inside top of the tube to hide the wadded wrapper beneath them.

Keeping your hand as it is, slide the tube over the opening, as if to let the soap fall into the net, and slide it back to the left. Lift the tube and make sure everybody sees it is empty. They think the soap is in the net. Drop your right hand, holding the tube, to your side a moment as you go on talking. Then bring that hand up to the cloth, catch the cloth under your thumb against the outside of the tube, and pull the cloth free of the elastic and completely away from the tray, showing there is nothing in the net or the tube, which you continue to hold up so the audience may see through it. When the trick is over, drop the cloth on the tray, put the tube on top of it, and secretly let the wrapper fall from your fingers inside the tube as you carry the tray away.

To set it up for the show, have the soap wrapper and tube

on the tray and the cloth in place over the elastic, and put the tray behind your screen on the prop table.

What you say and do:

MAGICIAN: (*Coming forward with tray.*) People often say they wish they were standing backstage so they could find out how the tricks are done. As a matter of fact, that would spoil all the fun ... but I've decided to let you in on the secret of this one. I'm going to give you a backstage view ... just as if you were seated behind me instead of out there where you are. First, I'll run through it, so you can see how it looks from the front.

(*Left hand holds tray. Right hand, fingers inside and thumb outside, holds up tube to show it empty, rests it on tray again.*)

This was worked out for a television soap commercial.

(*Right hand picks up soap, shows it, taps it on tray to make solid sound.*)

This is the hard soap ... all the rest of the commercial was soft soap.

(*Right hand puts soap inside tube.*)

It's a quick one, so watch.

(*Right hand slides tube over opening to let soap fall into net.*)

A little fiddling around, just to distract you.

(*Right hand slides tube back to left of tray. With fingers inside and thumb outside, right hand lifts tube and shows it empty.*)

And the soap is all gone ... just like on Saturday night ... I promised to show you how it was done and I will.

(*Faces left and holds tray well out from body so back of tray is toward audience.*)

Now you can pretend you're seeing the same thing from backstage.

(*Shows tube empty to imaginary audience at rear of stage, taps soap on tray, puts it into tube, moves tube over net so soap drops into it, moves tube back and shows it empty to imaginary audience at rear. Then faces front and smiles.*)

Awfully simple ... simply awful ... but you'll have to admit it does look convincing from out front.

(*Taps soap on tray, puts it into tube, secretly crushes wrapper. Holds fingers to conceal crushed wrapper against inside top of tube. Moves tube over net and slides it back to left of tray. Lifts tube to show it empty. As he continues speaking, right hand drops naturally to side with tube.*)

You'd be fooled, wouldn't you? But if you're going to try it yourselves to fool your friends, there's one thing I'd better warn you about. You have to be very careful not to lift the tray too high ... or the audience will see the soap in the net and that will give the whole trick away. If that happens, you have to make the soap disappear the hard way ... by magic!

(*Right hand nips cloth skirt and pulls it completely away from tray, revealing that net is empty and soap really has vanished. Same hand is holding up tube to show it also is empty. Left hand turns tray over to show both sides. Right hand drops cloth on tray, puts tube on it, and magician backs to left of screen, leaves tray on prop table and goes to right side table where props for next routine are set.*)

The Bewildered Milkman

HAVING fooled your audience by leading them to believe you were going to expose the secret of a trick, they will be doubly watchful this time. And you want them to be. Part of the success of this next routine depends on how convincing your acting is when it appears that you really have made a mistake.

You start showing a trick in which a milk carton passes back and forth from one tube to another, but your hand seems to slip so the spectators see you are really using two cartons. Having apparently blundered, you decide you might as well explain how the thing works. In the process, a third carton appears. Then it vanishes, the cartons stand on their heads, and finally one of them turns into a can of soup.

It is all accomplished by means of a cardboard shell which fits over one of the cartons. The shell is tricked in such a way as to resemble another carton of milk, either right side up or upside down, and the can has been hidden all the time inside one of the cartons.

What you need:

Four empty quart size cardboard milk cartons. These should be the kind of containers that have flat sides and a tent-shaped top.

One can of condensed soup. This must be of a size to fit loosely inside one of the milk cartons.

Two sheets of white poster board.

A roll of transparent plastic tape and a roll of black cloth adhesive tape.

White all-purpose glue, a ruler, pencil. and a razor blade in a holder.

How you make the props:

Cut a piece of poster board 8″ x 14″. Put it the long way on a table and lay one of the cartons on its side vertically on top of it. Bend the poster board around the carton to make a square-sided tube. Crease it at the bends so its sides are flat. Let the tube spring open slightly, so it is about ½″ wider than the milk carton. With the pencil, mark where the joining place should be glued to keep it this width. Put the milk carton aside and glue together the tube you have made.

Take two more milk cartons and cut each of them right in half at the center. Discard the top halves of both. Carefully cut the bottoms out of the remaining pieces and then cut open both pieces at their seams and flatten them out. Cut apart the four panels of one of these pieces along the creased lines that formed the four sides. Now glue one of these cut-in-half milk carton panels firmly to the bottom half of each of the four sides of the poster board tube you made. Glue them on in order so that they match the bottom half of one of the milk cartons.

Next turn the poster board tube around on your table so

that these four panels are upside down. Glue the matching four half-panels from the second cut-apart carton right side up, in their proper order, to the remaining spaces on the sides of the poster board tube. There is no need for the carton panels to match at the center of the tube since this part won't be seen. Run strips of transparent tape down all the edges so it overlaps them and holds everything smooth and tight. The result should be a topless and bottomless shell that looks like the bottom halves of two milk cartons put together upside down to each other.

Put the can of soup inside one of the remaining whole milk cartons. Take a short strip of transparent tape, fold one end back on itself, and then fasten the top of that carton together with the sticky part of the tape. This gives you a little tab that will let you pull the tape free quickly to open the carton. Drop this carton inside the shell you have made. Close the top of the other whole carton with transparent tape so the two look exactly alike.

Make two *round* covering tubes of poster board, each about 4″ in diameter and 12″ high. Fasten each of these together with black cloth adhesive tape and use strips of the tape to make decorative bands around the outside top, center and bottom of each tube.

How you use them:

Put a tube over one of the milk cartons. Grasp the tube lightly around its center and lift it a few inches to show the carton. Do the same thing again, but this time squeeze the tube with your thumb and fingers to hold the carton inside it as you lift. From the front, the carton seems to have disappeared from under the tube. Now put the second tube over the other carton and its covering shell. By grasping one of the tubes around the center with each hand, you can reveal either carton or keep it hidden inside its tube. Squeeze the right tube but don't squeeze the left as you lift them and the carton appears under the tube at the left. Lift them again and squeeze the left tube but not the right one and the carton appears under the tube at the right.

Try something else this time with only the tube that covers the carton and its shell. Grasp that tube around its center with your left hand and squeeze just enough to keep the shell inside it. Lift the tube and shell together up off the carton. Put the tube and hidden shell down on the table next to the carton. Then lift the tube a few inches without squeezing it and reveal the bottom half of the shell. To the audience, it looks as if another milk carton has appeared under the tube.

Next, to understand how you can seem to make a milk carton turn itself over inside the tube, start with one of the tubes over the carton and shell. Turn the tube upside down and steady it with your left hand grasped around its center. Now squeeze with your left hand as you lift the tube a few inches. The carton, of course, appears to be standing on its head. Slide the tube down to cover the carton and then lift the tube a few inches again, but this time don't squeeze the tube. The shell that shows at the bottom makes it seem that the carton has righted itself inside the tube. Lower the tube over the shell and then lift it a few inches again, squeezing it to raise the shell with it, and the bottle seems to be on its head once more.

To produce the can of soup, turn the tube right side up at the end of the previous moves. Reach into the top of it and secretly pull open the tab of tape as you draw the carton part way out of the top of the tube to show it. Slide the carton back down into the tube. Grasp the center of the tube with your right hand and put your left hand palm down over the

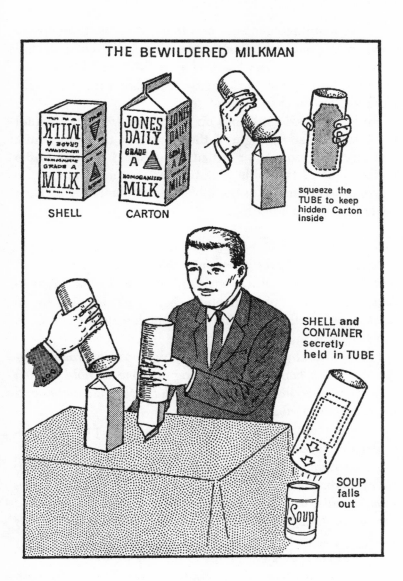

top of it. Keeping your left hand there, turn the tube upside down with your right hand, squeezing both the shell and carton. Move your left hand away a little and let the can drop out into it. Put the tube on the table with your right hand as you show the can of soup.

Here's how you set things up for the show: Stand behind the side table at the right of the stage. Put the empty milk carton at the front center of that table. Stand an empty tube at the right of the table. Put the carton that contains the can of soup at the left of the table. Slip its shell over it. Then cover it with the other tube.

What you say and do:

MAGICIAN: (*Standing behind table as he picks up milk carton and handles it as though it contained milk.*) A container of milk ... unfortunately there isn't enough to go around, or I'd offer you some. But I think we can have some fun with this milk ...

(*Puts carton back on table. Grasping one tube around center with each hand and squeezing left one to hold hidden carton and shell inside it, he lifts both tubes a few inches and lowers them to table again.*)

... and these two tubes ... the idea is to put the milk under this tube over here ...

(*Lifts right tube, covers carton with it, slides it back to right. Snaps fingers over one tube and then the other. Then grasps a tube with each hand and lifts them a few inches at the same time, squeezing right tube. Shows carton has changed places.*)

... and right away, it jumps to the other one.

(*Puts tubes down. Snaps fingers over them. Lifts both tubes, squeezing left, to show carton under right one.*)

Just as fast . . . the milk is back here again.

(*Lifts both tubes up and down together, alternately squeezing left or right, as carton seems to hop from one tube to the other.*)

Over here . . . over there . . . here . . . there . . .

(*Lifts both tubes up and down several times without squeezing either, thus revealing both cartons.*)

. . . back and forth, it goes.

(*For a moment, doesn't realize his "mistake." Then, holding both tubes up, glances down at both cartons. Quickly and nervously drops the tubes to cover them.*)

Oh . . . oh . . .

(*Looks out at audience, embarrassed.*)

I guess I goofed.

(*Runs index finger across throat, shakes head, then shrugs and smiles.*)

Well, there's no use trying to keep the truth from you now.

(*Lifts both tubes completely off cartons, squeezing left tube to keep shell hidden in it, and rests them on table.*)

I do have two containers of milk . . .

(*Picks them up, shows them, and puts them down again. Then lifts up both tubes, squeezing left one to hide shell. Puts those down.*)

. . . and the two tubes, of course.

(*With left hand, picks up carton, puts it down next to left tube.*)

This is the hidden one . . . when I cover the other one with its tube . . .

(*Right hand covers right carton with its tube.*)

. . . and have this container . . .

(*Touches carton that is next to left tube.*)

. . . hidden under the other tube . . .

(*Left hand picks up its tube, squeezing to keep shell hidden, and puts tube down again.*)

. . . it's no trick at all to make the milk seem to jump from here . . .

(*Right hand lifts its tube, squeezing to hide carton in it.*) . . . over to there.

(*Left hand lifts its tube a few inches, revealing bottom of shell, which looks like a third carton of milk. Both hands lower tubes to table. Then both hands lift again, left hand squeezing to hide shell. Carton seems to have jumped back to right.*)

And, of course, it seems to go, just as easily, right back again . . . Here and there . . . here and there.

(*Alternately lifts tubes, seeming to make carton hop back and forth, finally showing it under right tube and lifting that tube off it completely, resting tube behind carton.*)

Imagine the bewildered milkman if he saw something like that first thing in the morning.

(*Leaves things as they are, two cartons and two tubes visible, shell hidden in left tube, and steps around to the front of the table. Smiles as if routine were over, leaving audience puzzled over appearance and vanish of "third" carton.*)

Now that you all know exactly how it's done . . . promise me you won't tell anybody, will you?

(*If there is applause, he bows and takes it, waits for it to quiet.*)

Actually, these two containers of milk do work in sympathy.

(*Steps behind table again. Covers left carton with left tube and hidden shell. Turns that upside down. Grasps it with left hand around center of tube and steadies it there. With*

right hand, covers right carton. Right hand then grasps the
left side of its tube, turns that upside down with the carton
in it, and steadies it.)

Naturally, if you turn them both upside down, they look
like this.

(Both hands lift tubes a few inches, left hand squeezing
to keep shell hidden, showing both cartons standing on their
heads. Hands then lower tubes again.)

But if you turn just this one right side up . . .

(Right hand turns its tube over. Left hand stays as it is.)

. . . and use a little magic on the other one . . . then they are
both right side up.

(Both hands lift tubes a little without squeezing either.
Bottom of shell shows under left tube and looks as if carton
has righted itself.)

On the other hand, if you turn just this one upside down
and leave the other as it is . . .

(Right hand turns its tube upside down. Left hand stays
as it is.)

. . . they still show their magic bond of sympathy and both
containers of milk are upside down again.

(Both hands lift tubes a few inches, left hand squeezing
shell to keep it hidden. Hands then lower both tubes to rest
them on table. Right hand turns its tube upright and leaves
it that way. Right hand then comes over and grasps center
of tube left hand has been holding. Left hand goes under
bottom of that tube. Carrying tube, magician steps around
left side of table to stand in front of it.)

Truly, the real secret is that the containers can flip themselves over inside the tubes like acrobats . . .

(Right hand slides tube up, squeezing to hold shell in tube.

Left hand, under tube, supports upside down carton as it is shown.)

... quicker than you can say ...

(Right hand lowers tube and immediately lifts it a few inches again without squeezing, showing bottom of shell which looks like carton has righted itself.)

... allez ...

(Right hand lowers tube once more and immediately lifts it, squeezing to hide shell, showing carton upside down.)

... oops!

(Right hand squeezes to lift tube and hidden shell completely off carton and puts tube on table. Right hand drops to side. Left hand displays carton, turns it right side up, and drops it into top of tube on table so it slides down inside hidden shell. Then right hand reaches into top of tube, secretly pulls free tab of tape that has held carton shut, and immediately pulls carton part way out top of tube to show it again.)

As far as I'm concerned, I don't want milk at all.

(Right hand lowers carton into tube. Left hand goes palm down over top of tube. Right hand grasps tube and squeezes hard to hold both carton and shell in tube as both hands turn over and can of soup drops out into left hand. Right hand puts tube on table as left hand holds up can and shows it.)

I'll take soup!

(Bowing to his applause, magician steps back and exits behind back screen a moment, putting can on prop table and picking up tray with props from next routines. Immediately enters from other side of screen, carries tray to center table and begins following trick.)

A Trip to the Orient

WHILE each of the three following routines is different in effect, they have in common an Oriental atmosphere that builds toward the climax of your act. You can dress them up even more by getting into a colorful coolie coat and putting a tasseled Oriental skull cap on your head. These things, which can be on the prop table behind the screen, give you a quick change of costume with little trouble. When you finish the preceding routine, step behind the screen, put on the cap, slip into the jacket, pick up the tray and enter from the other side of the screen almost immediately. The costume isn't necessary, of course, but it will add to the entertainment value of your show.

In this first effect, you tear up two pieces of colored tissue paper and seem to transform them into a Japanese paper lantern. The lantern, weighted so it will open by itself, actually is concealed in a pocket of one of the papers, and is fixed so the torn pieces become what looks like a decorative knob at the bottom of it.

What you need:

A Japanese folding paper lantern, about 6″ in diameter.
A roll of ¾″ cloth or plastic adhesive tape.

Three flat lead curtain weights.

A sheet of black construction paper.

Black, or dark blue, tissue paper. The less easily this can be seen through, the better.

Red tissue paper.

Rubber cement, scissors, a pencil, and white all-purpose glue.

How you make the props:

Stack the three lead weights together and fasten them to the inside center of the bottom of the lantern with cross strips of the adhesive tape. If there is a bottom tassel on the lantern, remove and discard it. Place the lantern on the black construction paper and, with the pencil, draw a circle around the bottom. Cut out the circle, glue it to the bottom of the lantern, and trim it off evenly.

Cut a piece of the black or dark blue tissue 20″ long and 8″ wide. Lay it flat on a table. With rubber cement, coat a patch about 2″ in diameter on the center of the outside bottom of the lantern. Cement the lantern to the paper so it is centered about 1″ in from the right side. Make sure it sticks tightly to the paper. Then cut a second piece of the same dark tissue 8″ long and 8″ wide. Apply rubber cement around all four edges of it. Turn this piece over and cement it to the right end of the first piece, so it forms a pocket which has the lantern in the center. All edges of the two pieces should match neatly.

Finally cut a piece of red tissue 20″ long and 8″ wide, lay that on the table, and place the black strip evenly on top of it. Start at the right end and fold them together toward the left, making the first fold just past the concealed lantern. Continue folding to the left, creasing the folds as you go.

A TRIP TO THE ORIENT

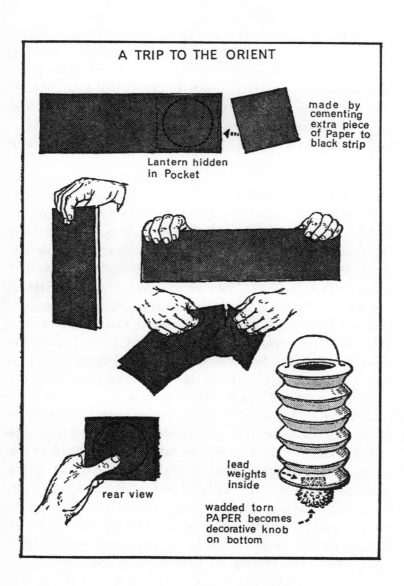

made by
cementing
extra piece
of Paper to
black strip

Lantern hidden
in Pocket

rear view

lead
weights
inside

wadded torn
PAPER becomes
decorative knob
on bottom

Turn the packet over and it will be in a position to begin the trick.

Since you probably will want a number of these, for practice and to have ready for your shows, it will save labor if you cut a quantity of the paper strips at the same time and buy enough lanterns to make up spare packets. The lanterns may be used over again, of course, for making up new sets of papers.

How you use them:

Put the packet on your table so the open ends are on top. With your right fingers and thumb, pick up the two ends together, give the packet a gentle shake, and it will unfold itself. Bring your left hand to the top and take the red paper with that hand. Hold your arms wide apart, letting one paper strip hang down from each hand, and show them that way. Bring the strips together with the red one at the front and hold them up with your right hand. Turn your hand to show the backs of the strips and then turn it to the front again, so they hang down the way they were, the red piece once more facing the audience.

Transfer both papers to the left hand, which takes them at the top. Run your right hand down the length of the strips to grasp them at the bottom and lift your right hand so the strips are horizontal in front of you. Show them that way a moment. Keeping your left hand as it is, remove your right hand from the papers. Now bring your right hand up to your left and tear both strips across. Put the torn pieces in front of the others, move your hands along and tear the strips once more, again putting the torn pieces at the front.

Continue tearing like this until you come to the pocket that conceals the lantern. This is now at the back of the torn

pieces. With your right hand, tear the pocket open wide.
Then, with both hands, crumple all the torn pieces around
to the front, crushing them into a tightly wadded ball. With
your right hand, grasp the little wire handle and let the lantern fall open. Hold it up and show it.

When you set things up for your show, simply have a prepared packet on a tray, with the exposed ends up so you can
grasp them quickly. The same tray, that you carry from behind the screen to your center table, will hold some of the
props for the routine that is to follow this one.

What you say and do:

MAGICIAN: (*Wearing coolie coat and Oriental skull cap,
approaches center table carrying tray and puts it down.*)
Now, a trip to the Orient . . . magic from Japan.

(*Right hand picks up papers and lets them fall open. Left
takes red strip at top and arms separate so a strip hangs from
each hand. Left hand brings red strip to front of right. Right
hand takes both strips, turns to show backs of them, and turns
them frontwards again.*)

This one is fun if you happen to be going to a Japanese
garden party.

(*Right hand lifts bottoms of strips so they are held horizontally stretched between both hands. Right hand drops its
ends and comes up to left hand. Tearing the strips across,
magician puts torn pieces in front.*)

Many pieces of paper . . .

(*Continues tearing until he comes to pocket concealing
lantern. Tears open pocket, crumples all torn pieces to front,
wads them into a tight ball.*)

. . . and just a touch of magic!

(*Right hand takes handle, lets lantern fall open and expand into view. Ball of torn pieces stuck to bottom looks like decoration.*)

Welcome to my Japanese garden.

(*Shows lantern a moment, takes applause, backs to screen and hangs lantern from picture hook at top of screen. Comes forward to center table, starting talk for next routine.*)

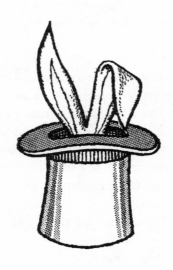

All the Rice in China

THIS WILL be your next-to-closing effect and should be the strongest spot in your show. It makes use of a magical theme with proven appeal, borrowing its basic plot from a trick that has long been a favorite with many magicians, "The Chinese Rice Bowls," but does not use any of the usual props. Part of it, in which a few handfuls of rice seem to increase in quantity until they spill over the sides of a bowl, is nothing but a plain bluff, since you never really show your audience how much rice you had in the first place. The rest of the props are not difficult to use and they will help you act out an entertaining story.

The action, as far as the magic is concerned, is that you pour a few handfuls of rice into a small round container, put the container into a tube, and it appears under a second tube that you previously have proven empty. The rice increases in quantity. But the audience wonders what is under the first tube, since you have failed to show that the container really disappeared from there. Lifting that tube, you reveal, not the duplicate container they think may be there, but a stemmed glass filled with water, which you spill out into a bowl.

What you need:

Two round cardboard containers with removable lids. One should be about 7″ high and 4½″ in diameter and the other about 6½″ high and 4″ in diameter, so that when the bottom is cut from the larger one the smaller one will fit up inside it. But they should be close enough in size so that when they are shown separately the audience will imagine they are identical. In your supermarket, you should be able to find round packages of cereal, such as those with oatmeal and corn meal, with containers that will serve. Failing that, two of the round metal cans, graduated in size, from a kitchen canister set will do as well. The bottom of the larger one may be removed with a can opener that leaves a clean and smooth edge. Instructions given here will be for making the props with cardboard containers, but you should have no trouble adapting them to the metal canisters if you decide to use those.

A small can of quick-drying black enamel and another of Chinese Red enamel.

A paint brush.

A sheet of black poster board and a sheet of green poster board.

A roll of 1½″ black cloth or plastic adhesive tape.

White all-purpose glue.

A stemmed glass or decorative clear goblet that stands about 6½″ high and has a top about 3″ in diameter.

A bowl about 2″ high and 3½″ in diameter. It will dress things up if this is Oriental in design.

A much larger bowl of somewhat similar design into which

you will pour the glass of water. This should be approximately 4″ high and 8″ in diameter.

Water to fill the glass.

Rice to fill the smaller container.

A metal tray with an edge about 1″ high. The high edge is to keep rice from spilling on the floor.

A pencil and scissors.

How you make the props:

Open both containers, by peeling their top lids free without tearing them, empty them and discard the contents. Put the lids aside. Cut away the entire bottom of the larger container and trim the bottom edge neatly so no tiny bits of rough cardboard remain. Paint the outsides of both containers Chinese Red. When they are thoroughly dry, paint a decorative black band ½″ wide around the bottom edge of each and also paint the entire bottom of the smaller one black. Use black paint to cover the outside of the top lid of the larger container and to paint both the inside and outside of the top lid of the smaller one. Let them dry and then firmly glue its top lid to the larger container so that it will remain fixed in place.

With the black poster board, make a tube about 12″ high and 4¾″ in diameter. The exact dimensions will depend on the size of the containers you are using. The tube should be about 5″ taller than the larger container and wide enough for that one to drop through it easily. Mark the joining place with a pencil and fasten the tube together with the cloth or plastic tape. Also run a length of tape down the inside seam of the tube so its interior will be perfectly smooth. For decoration, you can band strips of tape around the top and bottom of the tube, but don't turn them over those edges to the inside because that would keep the containers from falling through freely. Now make a second tube in the same way with the green poster board, but make its diameter a tiny bit smaller so you can nest it inside the black one for packing.

How you use them:

To go through the moves, set it up by putting the green tube, with the glass of water under it, on a table to your left. Have the large bowl beside that. Pour rice into the smaller container until it is nearly full and put the lid on it. Place that container and the black tube on the tray and put those on your center table. Drop the bottomless container down inside the tube. Have a few handfuls of rice in the smaller bowl and put that beside them.

Stand a little to the right of the center table. With your right hand, pick up the container from the tray and show it. Rest it on the table itself, just in front of the tray. Remove the lid. Scoop a few handfuls of rice from the bowl and let them trickle down into the container, which nobody should guess is already nearly filled with rice, and then put the lid back on it. With your left hand, grasp the tube close to the bottom, squeezing it to hold the bottomless container which is hidden inside it, and put it down over the smaller container at the front of the table.

Now, with your left hand near the top of it, slide the tube over the front edge of the table until your right palm can go under the bottom of it and remove it from the table. Keeping both hands in that position on the tube, tilt the top of the tube down forward until the nested containers slide through the tube away from your body. As they start to come out what is now the downward end of the tube, grasp the top container with your left hand and hold it. Tilt the tube

ALL THE RICE IN CHINA

TUBE tilted down and then up — secretly slides smaller container out of larger to fall to palm of Hand

smaller CONTAINER fits inside of bottomless larger one

RICE poured into BOWL

water !

upward slightly so the smaller container secretly slides back down inside the tube to rest against your right palm. As you turn toward the table, continue tilting the tube until it is upright on the palm of your right hand. Slide the bottom edge of the tube on the table from your right hand to leave the tube there and immediately lift the top container completely out of and away from the tube with your left hand. Hold your left hand so the top of that container is tilted toward the audience to keep them from seeing that it is bottomless.

You will want to practice these moves until you can do them smoothly. The whole thing takes only a moment. It is supposed to look as if you merely passed the container through the tube to show there could be nothing else inside the tube. The audience must think that the bottomless container you now have in your left hand is the same one you showed them originally, into which you poured a few handfuls of rice.

Carry that container, with its top still tilted toward the audience, over to the green tube on the other table. Drop it down into the tube. Because the container is bottomless, it falls over the glass of water and conceals it. Lift off the green tube to show the container there. Hold up the tube, show it empty, and cover the container with it again.

Go back to the black tube on the center table. Lift that and reveal the duplicate container. It looks as though the container had flown from one tube to the other. Remove its lid and slowly pour the rice into the bowl, holding the container high as you do. The rice overflows the bowl and spills over the tray so its quantity seems to have multiplied many times. Put the container down as though that were the end of the trick.

Some people in the audience may call out at this point that you forgot to show that the container was gone from under the green tube. Whether they do or not, you pretend to hear such a remark. Walk over to the green tube. Grasp it with your left hand around it, squeezing to hold the bottomless container that is hidden inside it. Lift it straight up and put it on the table. Pick up the glass of water, show it, and pour it into the bowl.

This is the set-up for the routine: The glass of water, with the green tube covering it, is on the left side table with the large bowl. The black tube with the bottomless container hidden inside it is on the high-edged tray. Also on the tray is the smaller container, nearly filled with rice, and the small bowl with rice in it. The packet of papers for the previous trick is with them and the tray is on your prop table. You bring the tray out to your center table before you change the torn papers into a lantern, so that when you actually start *All the Rice in China,* the tray with the props for it already is on your working table.

What you say and do:

MAGICIAN: (*Standing to right of center table.*) The story was told in ancient China, centuries ago, of a time of great famine when people were starving because the waters of the rivers had dried. According to the legend, they were saved from the drought that blighted the crops by the emperor's magician . . . and his magic rice.

(*Left hand scoops some rice from bowl and lets it trickle back again.*)

He kept his precious grains in a canister in a cupboard of the palace.

(Right hand picks up container from tray, shows it, puts it on table close to front edge, and removes lid.)

Hardly more than a few handfuls . . .

(Right hand scoops a little rice from bowl and lets it trickle into container. Repeats this several times, then puts lid on container.)

. . . but with his magic . . . it was enough to feed the nation . . . even though the rivers had run dry.

(Passes container through tube in the way practiced, really substituting duplicate bottomless container for it.)

Whenever rice was needed, he would dispatch the canister . . . with just a few handfuls in it . . . by special messenger to wherever in China it was wanted.

(Left hand holds tilted container high as magician walks swiftly to left side table. Drops container into green tube and lifts tube off to show it. Shows tube empty.)

When that precious little of the rice reached the planters, something truly magical happened. For every single grain planted . . .

(Covers container again with green tube. Walks back to center table and continues speaking.)

. . . a thousand and a hundred thousand grains would fill the fields beyond it. The same magic would transport the canister itself from the distant places it had been . . . back to the palace cupboard of the royal magician.

(Lifts black tube to reveal container apparently has returned.)

The legend was . . . that it was carried by an invisible chariot drawn by a swarm of golden butterflies.

(Smiles and picks up container, removing lid.)

Now that part may not be true . . . but there was always rice again when the royal magician wanted it to send to other places. Even on his palace shelf ... it multiplied in great quantity so that instead of a few precious grains ... there were thousands.

(*Slowly pours rice from container into bowl. Flood of rice continues, spilling over bowl and tray.*)

And that was the story that was told in China long ago.

(*Acts as though routine were finished. Puts down container, smiles, lifts hands to encourage applause, bows as if other tube were completely forgotten. Audience may call out to remind him. Whether there are calls or not, he pretends to hear such a remark. Frowns, looks out to audience.*)

What? ... what's that? Oh, the other tube over there. I did forget to show you that, didn't I?

(*Walks swiftly to left table.*)

You think the canister of rice is still here? But it couldn't be ... it's over there.

(*Puts hand on green tube.*)

No, not rice ... something far more precious than rice in a land where all the rivers had run dry.

(*Quickly lifts tube. Reveals glass of water. Puts tube down, holds glass high, splashes water into bowl.*)

Just water ... pure water ... to make the rice grow!

(*Puts down glass, takes bows, immediately goes into closing routine.*)

A Feast of Lanterns

YOUR FINAL routine is done rapidly and entirely in pantomime, bringing one surprise after another, and ending in
a burst of color as the curtains close. You pick up a bucket,
prove it empty, pour water into it, and quickly produce six
silk scarves of different colors, then half a dozen paper lanterns which you hang from the hooks at the top of the back
screen, and finally an Oriental fan.

Then you pour the water out of the bucket into a bowl.
Fanning the bucket, you walk to the front of the stage where
you pull a ribbon of changing colors from it. You catch the
ribbon with the fan and swirl it around in a widening rainbow of color to end the show.

Everything is contained within the bucket, which is tricked
to hold the water away from the things secretly packed inside
it. Actually, there is hardly anything you have to learn to
do, except to play the part of the magician well and build
the kind of audience excitement that should bring you good
applause.

What you need:

A large cardboard paint tub, the gallon size, not the quart size that was used for *The Magic Tax*. It should be approximately 8″ high and 9″ in diameter at the top, tapered to a diameter of about 6½″ at the bottom.

The sort of a large paper cup used at soda fountains for milk shakes.

Ten 3-yard lengths of ½″ wide rayon ribbon in as many different bright colors as you can find.

Five Japanese folding paper lanterns, each about 6″ in diameter.

An Oriental folding fan, small enough to fit well inside the bucket.

Six 24″ Japanese silk scarves in various colors.

Red plastic cloth adhesive tape about 1″ wide.

A can of Chinese Red spray paint.

Fifteen flat lead curtain weights.

A spool of colorless nylon thread and a needle.

Scotch tape, a pencil, and a razor blade in a holder.

How you make the props:

Take the large paper cup, measure 6″ up from the bottom of it, draw a line there and cut around it horizontally. Discard the cut-off top part. Put the remaining part of the cup into the cardboard paint bucket and against one side of it so that the bottom of the cup is 1″ above the inside bottom of the bucket. With the red plastic cloth tape, fasten the cup firmly in that position by running several strips of the tape from near the inside top of the bucket vertically right down the side to the inside bottom of the cup. Reinforce it by fastening other strips of tape around the outside of the cup

A FEAST OF LANTERNS

BUCKET turned upside down to prove empty

Water poured in from BOWL

SILK SCARVES pulled out

weighted paper LANTERNS taken out and FAN produced

WATER poured back into BOWL

WATER poured into hidden CUP

RIBBON comes from center of COIL

hidden CUP fastened inside of BUCKET

LANTERN

TAPE

horizontally to hold it tightly to the side of the bucket. When that has been done, spray the entire bucket, inside and out, with the Chinese Red paint and let it dry thoroughly.

Sew the lengths of ribbon together end to end with the colorless nylon thread. Vary the order of the colors and make sure the lengths are firmly sewn to each other. Now take one end of the entire streamer of ribbon and roll it around two fingers until you have the start of what will be a flat coil of ribbon with an opening about 1″ in diameter in its center. Straighten the sides of the coil as you roll it. Once the coil has been well started, you will find you can roll it more smoothly by holding it upright on your left palm with the thumb and first finger of that hand through the center hole while you turn it with your right hand. When you come to the end, fasten it with Scotch tape. After the ribbon has been used in a show, it should be pressed before rolling it into a coil again for the next show.

Fasten three of the flat curtain weights, stacked together, inside the bottom of each paper lantern with cross pieces of the plastic cloth tape, as you did with the lantern used in *A Trip to the Orient.*

How you use them:

When you are sure the red paint is dry, start to load the bucket by sliding the flat coil of ribbon in under the cup. The coil lies on the bottom of the bucket. Pull an end of ribbon from the *center* of the coil, bring that end up to the side of the bucket opposite the cup and about 2″ down from the top and fasten it there with a tab of Scotch tape. Make the tab by folding part of the tape back on itself so you can free the ribbon end quickly when the time comes.

Next put the fan into the bucket. Then the lanterns, stacked together and on edge. The silk scarves are packed around the rest of the things and should hold them so you can turn the bucket upside down without spilling anything out. Start by putting in one end of a scarf and folding it down upon itself in loose accordion pleats, then put another in that way, and so on until they are all in place. Nothing should show above the top of the bucket and everything should be clear of the paper cup attached inside it.

Set things up by putting the bucket on the floor next to your left side table. The side of the bucket with the paper cup should be toward the table. You will use the bowl and water from *All the Rice in China*. The water, which seems to be poured into the bucket, really goes into the paper cup attached inside it. When you pour it, the bucket will be on the table. You will want to practice pouring the water from the bowl into the hidden cup so you can learn to hold the bowl fairly high and still not splash any of the things hidden in the bucket. The routine is performed silently, immediately after you have finished *All the Rice in China*.

What you do:

MAGICIAN: (*With left hand, picks up bucket from floor, turns it with mouth toward rear until it is upside down. Taps bottom gently with right hand to "prove" by magician's logic that bucket is empty. Turns it upright and puts it on left side table. Both hands pick up bowl and pour water into hidden cup inside bucket, holding bowl high so stream of water is clearly seen. Hands put bowl back on table.*

Magician takes step forward, dramatically claps hands together, steps back and looks into bucket, shakes head in disappointment. Claps hands again, looks into bucket, turns to audience and nods as if magic has been successful this time.

Reaches into bucket and pulls out one corner of a scarf, slowly pulls it completely into view, holds it stretched between hands and shows it. Tosses it across top of back screen and leaves it there. Produces another scarf the same way. Then produces remaining scarves more quickly, tossing each to hang over top of screen.

Looks into bucket, claps hands together smartly. Takes out first lantern, holding it by handle and letting it expand itself as weights in bottom pull it open. Hangs lantern on one of picture hooks at top of screen. Takes out other lanterns and hangs each of those. Produces fan, snaps it open, fans self. Rests fan on table a moment. Takes bucket between both hands, holds it high, tips it to left so water runs out of hidden cup and splashes back into bowl on table.

His left hand takes bucket by its top. Right hand picks up fan. Magician walks briskly to front and center of stage, fanning bucket. Tucks fan under left arm to hold it. With right hand, reaches into bucket, secretly pulls free tab of tape, withdraws end of ribbon with a forward throwing motion that swirls it into the air. Does that several times, pulling out ribbon in swirling lengths. Right hand takes fan from under left arm. Catches ribbon against fan and waves fan in widening clockwise circles, swirling ribbon out of bucket faster and faster in a whirl of changing colors. Curtains close slowly as he spins out the ribbon. He puts bucket on center table. Curtains snap open quickly again as he bows and takes his applause.)

The Stage Show Set-up

HERE, IN brief, is the set-up for the stage show:
Center table is front of stage. Side tables are on a line, left and right, slightly to rear. Screen is at center back, with picture hooks along its top. Prop table stands behind it with clearance to walk between this table and rear of stage.

Props for *Hawaiian Magic* are on center table. On the right side table is the set-up for *The Bewildered Milkman*. Behind the screen on the prop table are the props for *No Soap*, a coolie jacket and Oriental skull cap, and a tray which holds the paper lantern packet for *A Trip to the Orient* and the black tube, container, and bowl of rice for *All the Rice in China*.

On the left side table are the green tube, with the glass of water loaded under it, plus the large water bowl for *All the Rice in China*. Beside the table, on the floor, is the loaded bucket for *A Feast of Lanterns*.

You will need someone to work the curtains for you and he should be instructed to pull them open with a snap at the beginning of the show, to close them very slowly at the end, and then to snap them open quickly again for you to take your applause.

ACT THREE

Magic in a Briefcase

THIS IS a show you can give under nearly any performing conditions. You can set it up at home, pack it into a briefcase, and keep it always ready for whenever you may be called upon to perform without much advance notice. When you get to where you are going to do your magic, you can take the tricks right out of your briefcase and do them without any further set-up or delay.

Everything needed for the show will fit into one briefcase or attaché case. You can make use of whatever small table may be available, or even a piano top, or a couple of chairs, if there is no table. As you perform, the things for each trick are taken from the briefcase, and then are put back into it when you finish with them, so there is nothing to pack away afterwards.

The tricks have been chosen and routined so they can be done either on a level with your audience, as in a club show, or else on a small platform, with little to worry about as far as the angles of performance are concerned. It is the sort of an act that will let you accept a last-minute invitation to give a show, and just pick up your briefcase and go.

The Instant Shopper

THE UNUSUAL articles you produce in this opening effect should amuse your audience and get the show off to a good start. While there is no great mystery involved, the element of surprise is strong, and it should help you win full attention and make the audience wonder what you will do next.

You show a sheet of newspaper, fold it, snap your finger against it to tear the paper, and produce a nylon stocking. Turn it over, tear it again, and you have a tube of toothpaste. Another fold and another tear and you're holding a slice of bread. Finally, you have a handful of dollar bills. The various items fit the theme of the story you tell as you produce them.

The secret depends on the use of a duplicate sheet of newspaper, cut and pasted to the original in such a way as to form hidden pockets that conceal the things.

What you need:

A woman's nylon stocking.

An empty toothpaste or shaving cream tube.

111

A slice of bread. This should be stale, so that it has become hard. You may prefer to toast it.

Half a dozen "play money" dollar bills.

Two identical copies of a standard size newspaper, so you will have duplicate pages.

All-purpose white glue.

Scissors, a pencil, pliers, and a dull-bladed table knife.

How you make the props:

With the knife, pry open and remove the clamp that holds together the bottom of the toothpaste tube. Push the blade up inside, scrape out any toothpaste that remains, stuff the tube with bits of crumpled newspaper, and use the pliers to put the clamp back on and seal the bottom together again. You will want a tube that isn't bulky, but one which also has a little body and isn't crushed completely flat. Its light weight is its main advantage as a prop.

Take two duplicate double sheets of newspaper (four pages each). Open out one of them and lay it on a clean floor or large table that will give you a smooth, flat and roomy working surface. With the pencil, lightly draw a vertical line down the center of the left-hand page. Then draw a light horizontal line across the middle of the same page.

You now have marked off four squares. Place the partly flattened toothpaste tube in the center of the top left square. Fold the stocking flat, don't bunch it, and lay that in the center of the top right square. Put the "dollar bills" in the center of the bottom left square and the slice of bread in the center of the bottom right one.

Cut the matching page from the duplicate newspaper. Trim off the top, sides and bottom borders of that page right along the edges of its printed matter. Turn it over and coat a 1″ wide stripe of glue around all the edges and then down the center vertically and across the middle horizontally. Hold the cut piece right side up and glue it over the original paper so that it matches exactly. Make sure all the edges and the divisions between the squares are tightly stuck and let the paper dry a few minutes.

Now close the paper from left to right. Fold it again horizontally on its natural center crease and then vertically fold the right half *back under* the left. Gently crumple the whole paper a little between your hands and smooth it out again so it looks a bit wrinkled, which helps to hide the small bulges where things are concealed.

How you use them:

Hold the folded paper in your left hand. Grip the top left corner and gently shake the paper open. Take the top right corner with your right hand and release the paper from your

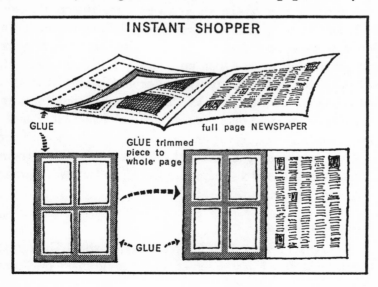

left hand. Turn your right hand to show the other side of the paper. Bring your left hand up again and open out the paper to hold it between your hands. Holding it that way, turn your body far enough to the left to let the audience see the back of the opened paper briefly. Then face front and fold it the way it was originally.

Rest the folded paper flatly on the open palm of your left hand. Your left thumb should grip its left edge to hold it there. Snap your right finger hard against the paper to tear through it and let the stocking pop into view. This snapping is done by springing the tip of your index finger from the ball of your thumb in the way you might shoot a "spitball" with them, but if it gives you trouble simply poke a hole in the newspaper with your index finger. Show the stocking and drop it on the table.

Turn the folded paper over to the left and rest it flatly again on the palm of your left hand. Snap your finger through the second pocket of the paper to produce the toothpaste. Hold that up long enough for everyone to see it well. Turn the paper back the way it was originally and rest it once more on your flat left palm. Open out the top folds, left to right, and bring the right half down *under* and back to the left. With the paper flat on your left hand, break through it with your right finger and take out the bread and show it. Finally turn the paper over, rest it on your left hand, and snap your right finger against it to reveal the "dollar bills." Show them a moment and then toss them into the air to let them shower down around you.

What you say and do:

MAGICIAN: (*Enters with briefcase under arm.*) Have you ever thought how just a touch of magic could make our lives a lot easier?

(*Puts briefcase flat on table, opens it and takes out news-paper.*)

How many times have you seen things advertised in the paper that you thought of buying and then forgot about by the time you finally went shopping?

(*Unfolds paper, shows it on all sides, folds it again and rests it on palm of left hand.*)

I've been working on a magical invention I call instant shopping. Let's say you see an ad in the paper for stockings ...

(*Snaps right finger through paper, stocking pops into view, and he pulls it out to show it.*)

... a touch of magic and the stockings are right at hand ... or suppose a big sale of cosmetics is advertised.

(*Snaps finger through paper, produces toothpaste, and shows it.*)

No rush ... no crowds ... delivered right to your home just as quick as a wish. I can't understand why advertisers don't use magic. Think of all the extra sales they would make if they could cash in on that kind of impulse buying ... stockings ... cosmetics ...

(*Casually, he flicks finger through paper again, produces bread and shows it.*)

... food ... and the best part of instant shopping is ... that with magic ...

(*Snaps finger through paper, takes out bills and shows them, tosses them high into air so they shower down around him as he finishes speaking.*)

... you'd always have the money to pay for it all!

(*Puts torn paper and things back into briefcase, on top side of partition that separates props still to be used from those already used, as will be explained later, and starts his next routine.*)

Blue Ribbon Magic

YOU'VE introduced yourself in a novel and amusing way, without doing anything so startling or sensational that you will have trouble topping it to build increasing interest in the rest of your show. But, having gained attention, you now have to hold it with something that happens rather quickly to promise that there are more surprises to come.

The next routine will give you some colorful and visual magic, with a very simple plot that is easy for everyone to follow. A blue ribbon vanishes from a folder in one hand and appears, instantly and visibly, linked to a yellow ribbon you are holding up in your other hand. The trick makes use of a rather interesting double folder, with a section that locks itself in a simple manner to conceal anything put inside it. It is a prop you will be able to use in other tricks you make up, for instance in changing one card for another.

As for the ribbon that appears linked within the other one, it is a duplicate, folded in such a way that your fingers hide it. But there is a bit of a trick to the folding and also to the method of keeping it set until you are ready to use it.

117

What you need:

Two one-yard lengths of 1″ wide blue rayon ribbon.

A one-yard length of 1″ wide yellow rayon ribbon.

A large bulldog clip. This is the clamp-type clip often used for holding papers to a clipboard.

A sheet of red poster board.

Double-stick transparent tape, the kind that is sticky on both sides.

Red plastic ¾″ adhesive tape.

Scissors.

How you make the props:

From the red poster board, cut three pieces, each 8½″ x 4″. Put them on the table in a vertical row, one under another, so their wide edges almost touch. Hinge the three together with horizontal strips of red tape, allowing a little space between them so all the panels will fold easily on their hinges. Reinforce the hinges at the back with the tape. Then use strips of it to make borders that frame all edges of each individual panel, front and back.

With the three panels hinged together and opened out flat, bend the top one back on its hinge so it goes *under* the center panel. On the bottom panel, put strips of double-stick tape right over the red border tape at both sides and along the bottom. The double-stick tape should not be wider than the red tape at any point because it must not touch the cardboard itself when the folder is closed.

Next knot the ends of a blue ribbon together to form a loop, then thread the yellow ribbon through it and knot the ends of that so the two loops are linked. Hold up the yellow loop so the blue one hangs from it and pull the blue one

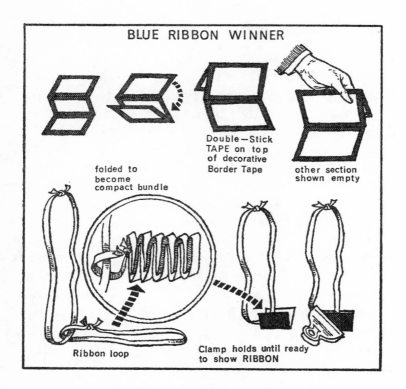

BLUE RIBBON WINNER

folded to
become
compact bundle

Double—Stick
TAPE on top
of decorative
Border Tape

other section
shown empty

Ribbon loop

Clamp holds until ready
to show RIBBON

around until its knot is about ½″ from the bottom of the
yellow loop. Put them that way on the table. Move the blue
ribbon up until it is at a right angle to the yellow one. Flatten
the part where the two join. Starting there, fold the doubled
blue ribbon back on itself. Fold it in flat and small accordion
pleats right on the bottom of the yellow loop. Finally, take
the spring clamp so its handle is toward the left and clamp
the ribbons to hold them in place until you are ready to show
the trick.

How you use them:

To make the ribbon disappear, start by holding the folder
open like a tray on the palm of your left hand, with the

folded-under double section at the rear and the opening to that part on the tips of your left fingers. Pick up the duplicate blue ribbon with your right hand. Hold it above the folder so the bottom end of the ribbon touches its center and let it drop. All the ribbon should fall within the panel borders.

With your left thumb, shut the folder. Bring your right hand to the front of it, grasp it there between your thumb and fingers, and squeeze it as you pick it up. The double-stick tape will stick those edges together. Without changing the position of your right thumb and fingers, turn that hand to the right and hold up the folder to show it. This brings one of the narrow edges to the top. Grasp that edge with your left fingers and squeeze again. At the same time, move your right hand to the narrow edge at the bottom and squeeze there as both hands turn the folder between them so it is held horizontally.

Turn the panel now facing front so it is toward the floor and put the folder on the table for a moment. All of this should look as if you merely picked it up from your left hand, showed it casually and placed it on the table. If you were performing the routine, you would need both hands at this point to remove the yellow ribbon from your briefcase, which is the reason for resting the folder on the table. But for now, let's go on with the vanish of the blue ribbon. Take the folder from the table so it rests on the palm of your left hand, with its open part still at the bottom and toward the heel of that hand. Slide your left thumb into the open part of the folder. Holding it with your thumb, flip the folder open so the bottom panel hangs down. The ribbon has vanished. By turning your left hand, you can show both sides of the folder.

When you want to use the folder again for another show, gently pull apart the stuck panels and separate them. Because

the double-stick tape fastens itself to sections of the red border tape, it will come free quite easily without tearing the
poster board. You will have to renew the double-stick tape
from time to time. When you start the trick, make sure the
folder panel is not stuck shut. It will be set up in your briefcase in a way to prevent its sticking, but it is wise to check
before taking it out.

For the other part, in which the blue ribbon appears linked
with the yellow one, you will have the clamped ribbons set
inside your briefcase at the start. Reach in with both hands.
Slip your right fingers inside the yellow loop and put your
right thumb on the folded bundle of blue ribbon. With your
left hand, remove the clamp and leave that in the briefcase.
This takes only an instant.

Close your right fingers around the yellow loop to hide
the blue ribbon and bring your hand out of the briefcase.
Show the yellow one and pull the loop through your right
hand, back and forth, a few times. Turn the back of your
right hand to the audience. Give the yellow ribbon a little
downward shake and open your right fingers slightly to release the blue one. It will drop into view and hang from the
bottom of the yellow loop. When you perform the routine,
your left hand flips open the folder to show the blue ribbon
gone at the same moment that your right hand releases its
duplicate, so that it appears hanging suddenly from the loop.

Set things up for the show by fixing the looped ribbons
and clamping them. Then open the sticky side of the folder,
put the clamped ribbons into it, close it loosely and wind the
other blue ribbon around the folder. Tuck the end of the
ribbon under its winding to hold it in place. This keeps the
sides of the folder apart so they won't stick. Pack it into your
briefcase that way. When you're ready to show the trick,

reach into your briefcase, put your right thumb inside the folder, dump the clamp out the side of it, and take out the folder and ribbon.

What you say and do:

MAGICIAN: I recently was awarded a blue ribbon.

(*Reaches into briefcase, removes folder and ribbon, unwinds ribbon.*)

The blue ribbon of the magicians' club . . . first prize.

(*Holds up ribbon, shows it, then opens folder.*)

Naturally, I'm rather proud of this, so I have a little case to keep it in . . . I wouldn't want anything to happen to it.

(*Drops ribbon into folder, closes folder, secretly sticks sides together in showing it, and rests folder momentarily on table.*)

It doesn't often happen, but the same magic also won me the second place award.

(*Reaches into briefcase, sets yellow ribbon in right hand, removes ribbon and holds it up.*)

It took the yellow ribbon as well as the blue.

(*Pulls yellow loop back and forth through right hand. Left hand then picks up folder, ready to flip it open, while right continues to display yellow loop.*)

I'm afraid I can't do it for you here tonight. As a matter of fact, it isn't the sort of thing that's ever likely to happen again. But I'll tell you about it. You see, I was doing a simple little trick in which I held a piece of blue ribbon in this hand and a yellow one in this hand . . .

(*Holds hands high and looks from one to the other as he speaks.*)

. . . and then something happened that I still don't understand. The ribbon took off by itself and flew through the air. What was so magical about it was that it happened right before their very eyes. Maybe you can imagine . . . how it looked.

(*Flips open folder and at same time makes ribbon appear linked in yellow one. Looks with surprise from empty folder to ribbon.*)

Well, what do you know . . . it did happen again!

(*Shakes his head, drops ribbons into folder, smiles to audience.*)

I didn't believe it myself the first time.

(*Puts things away in partitioned briefcase and begins talk for next effect.*)

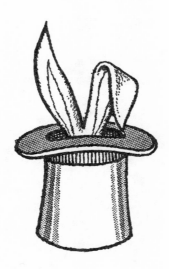

A Visit from Houdini

YOU ARE now going to stage a mock spirit seance to the extent of producing supposedly ghostly writing on a school slate as part of a routine that will give you a chance to tell your audience some interesting things about the greatest magical showman who ever lived, Harry Houdini. While this part of your show will depend on strong presentation to put it across effectively, the magic involved also should puzzle people and leave them with something to think about.

This version of the slate writing trick makes use of a bold subterfuge in which the secret device you use is prominently displayed before the audience, but in such a way that there is no reason to suspect it. A cardboard flap covers the previously written "spirit message" so the slate may be shown originally with no writing on it. The flap itself then becomes one of two signs that you set up to add a humorous note to the proceedings. As a result, there is nothing to hide once the trick is underway and nothing to dispose of at its ending.

What you need:

A set of alphabet stencils that will let you make letters 1¼″ high. These are available in most variety and stationery stores.

Two menu holders, the kind used for holding menus upright on restaurant tables and soda fountain counters. These have a metal clip attached to a small base and are sold in various styles by restaurant supply houses. You may be able to purchase some from a nearby restaurant or drug store. They are needed to hold two signs upright, so any small stands that will accomplish that purpose will serve as well.

A shot glass.

White chalk.

A 9″ x 12″ clasp-type manila envelope.

Black poster board.

A few sheets of white typewriter paper.

A slate that will fit into the envelope. This should be the usual "school slate" with a wooden frame. Instructions given here are for a slate 8¾″ x 6¾″, including a wooden frame that is 1″ wide. The writing surface is 6¾″ x 4¾″. But any slate of approximate size will do.

Scissors, white all-purpose glue, and a black felt-tip marking pen.

How you make the props:

Measure the writing surface of the slate, inside the wooden frame, and cut two pieces of black poster board just a trifle smaller. Either of them should fit easily over the slate's writing surface to cover it completely and yet fall out of the frame if the slate is turned over.

Take one of these pieces of poster board, lay it on a sheet

of white typewriter paper, and lightly mark around it with pencil to give you the size of the signs you are going to make. One sign will read: QUIET PLEASE. There should be one word on each line, horizontal across the long width. With a pencil, lightly mark guide lines for the lettering and then stencil the letters on the white paper with the black felt-tip marking pen. When the sign is dry, glue the paper to one side of the piece of black poster board and trim it neatly around the edges. The second sign, to be made in the same way, should read: SPOOKS AT WORK! Again, it should be spaced so there is one word to a line, and glued when dry

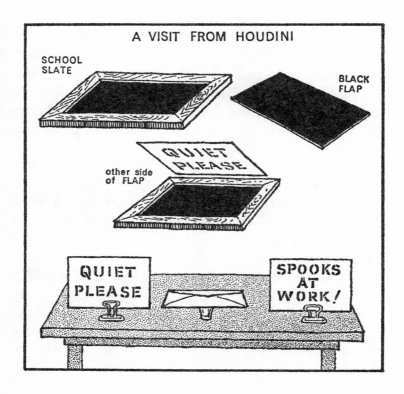

to the back of the second piece of poster board, with all edges trimmed.

How you use them:

Turn the slate so its short ends are horizontal. With the chalk, print this message on the slate in wavering letters as large as you can make them:

SORRY
CAN'T
BE
WITH YOU
—HOUDINI

Cover the writing with the SPOOKS AT WORK! sign so the black side of it faces out. Rub this with chalk and then wipe it off to give it a more slate-like appearance. This should now look like a plain surface of the slate with no writing on it. By holding the slate so that either thumb lightly presses against the flap, you can handle the slate quite freely and show that it is apparently blank on both sides.

Put the large envelope, back downward, on a table. Slide the QUIET PLEASE sign into the envelope with its lettering face up. Put the slate, with its flap side up, into the envelope on top of the sign. Now put the shot glass, the chalk, and the two menu clips in the front part of the envelope and fasten the clasp.

This is the way things will be set for the show. Everything is in the envelope when you pack it into your briefcase, so the entire effect is self-contained and you won't have to hunt around for the various props. Having the other things in the envelope also gives you a logical excuse for the moves you will make in handling the slate.

To run through what you will do, start by opening up the clasp and putting the envelope flat on the table, with its rear side down. With your left hand at its top, lift the envelope a little so you can look into it. Reach in with your right hand, remove the shot glass and put it on the front part of the table. Take out the chalk and place that in the glass. Reach in with your right hand again, make sure the flap is in position so it covers the writing on the slate, press your thumb against it lightly and take out the slate. There's no need to hurry. Bouncing around in the envelope, the flap may have come off the slate, so take time to be sure it is in place before you remove the slate.

Let the envelope fall flat on the table and leave it there a moment. Hold up the slate and make sure everybody sees both sides are blank. You will now ask some person in the audience to call out his initials so you can mark them on the slate. Hold it with the flap side to the rear and mark the initials in large letters on the front (non-flap) writing surface. Show both sides again.

Now hold the slate so the flap side is down and the initials are up. Slide it into the envelope. Immediately take out the two metal menu clips and stand one at each side of your table. Then take out the sign, together with the flap, which will have fallen from the slate frame inside the envelope so it is sign-side up. Clip the QUIET PLEASE sign into the menu holder to your right and the SPOOKS AT WORK! sign into the menu holder at your left. This one really is the flap of the slate, but it looks like the other sign and by boldly putting it on display you have gotten rid of the flap.

There is nothing left in the envelope now but the initialed slate with the message written on it. Close the clasp of the envelope, rest it flat on top of the shot glass, and go on with your talk. If you are working on a level with the audience, instead of putting the envelope on the shot glass, carry it to the person in the audience who called out his initials and have him hold it. Actually, the trick is already done and there is no secret left for anybody to discover, but in the routine you will be just starting the build-up.

Finally have the person holding the envelope open it and discover the "ghostly message," or if it is resting on the shot glass, you open it yourself and reveal what is written on the slate. The audience can look over the slate and the envelope all they wish, but there is nothing for them to learn. When the trick is over, unclip the signs and put them and everything else back into the briefcase and go on with the next routine.

What you say and do:

MAGICIAN: (*Speaks sincerely, in serious manner, setting the tone for what is to come.*) If you ask the average person to name a magician, the name he'll give you will be ... Houdini.

(*Takes envelope from briefcase and puts it on table.*)

Harry Houdini died in 1926. In terms of theater-going audiences, that's a whole generation ago. But he has become a legend, the greatest showman since P. T. Barnum ... It isn't true that his secrets died with him. Most magicians know how he performed his marvelous jail escapes and other magic, but none can do them with the daring and showmanship that was Houdini's.

His real name was Ehrich Weiss. His family was forced to flee from Hungary when he was a baby and he was brought to Wisconsin where he grew up. He learned the secrets of a locksmith for whom he worked, learned showmanship through long years of appearing in circuses, carnivals and dime museums before he achieved his great fame. He took his stage name from a French magician, Robert-Houdin. By adding an "I" it became ... Houdin ... eye ... because he hoped to become as great a magician as the celebrated French conjuror who was his boyhood idol.

(*While he is speaking, magician unfastens clasp of envelope, removes shot glass and puts it at front of table, drops chalk into shot glass, rests envelope on table again, taking his time with these things, but indicating something interesting is to come.*)

Houdini spent much of his time and energy fighting fraudulent spirit mediums, exposing those who used the tricks and secrets of magic to pose as real mediums and prey upon the bereaved ... fake spiritualists who pretended supernatural powers to conjure up the spirits of the departed so as to take money from those who had lost loved ones ... Houdini battled against them in cities across the land, testified at Congressional hearings, seeking laws to end the frauds. And yet, his was a life-long search in which he hoped he would find the proof of true spiritualism. What he fought against was not spiritualism itself, but the fakers among sincere spiritualists. Houdini exposed and ridiculed them, by using his skill as a magician to duplicate their ghostly manifestations.

(*Picks up envelope.*)

Let's pretend ... just for fun, of course ... that we're all at a spirit seance ... and the spirit of Houdini is with us.

(*Takes out slate and shows both sides of it.*)

Spiritualism had a great vogue in upstate New York in the 1800s ... at a time when slates like this were commonly used by every boy and girl who went to school. That is why mediums for years have been using school slates in their seances to record messages from the spirits.

(*Points to some man in the audience.*)

Will you, sir, call out your initials, please?

(*Writes them on front surface of slate. Shows slate both sides again and slides it into envelope, flap side down. Immediately brings out the two menu clips and stands one at each side of table.*)

If we're going to hold a seance, we'd better put up a couple of road signs ... you never know how thick the traffic in ghosts will get.

(*Puts the two signs in their holders.*)

Will you, sir, take this envelope containing the slate on which your initials are marked.

(*Takes envelope to man and has him hold it. Returns to face audience. Speaks dramatically.*)

Pretend with me, will you? Just imagine that all of us here tonight ... are seated around a table, holding hands. And the medium shows his slate, as I have done. He talks of ghostly visitors ... the lights go low ... we are in the dark.

(*Silent a moment, he then speaks in a loud whisper.*)

There is only the sound of our breathing ... but then ... then ... a tiny scratching, a scraping as if chalk were passing over the surface of a slate. Our spines tingle ... then all is quiet once more.

(*Claps hands suddenly, speaking in a startlingly loud voice.*)

Lights on! The seance has ended!

(*Points to man holding envelope.*)

Did you feel any ghostly stirrings? No? But then, you'd hardly feel a ghost. Open up the envelope, sir. Look at the slate inside it ... is there a message?

(*Hurries to man holding slate.*)

There is? There's something written on it? Your initials,

of course . . . are they still there? But the message, what does it say?

(*Takes the slate from him and reads the message aloud for those not close enough to see the words.*)

"Sorry can't be with you . . . Houdini."

(*Holds slate high and shows the writing on it.*)

Well, I'm sorry, too, that Houdini couldn't visit us to-night . . .

(*Smiles.*)

. . . but at least . . . he was here in spirit!

(*Takes applause. Returns to table. Looks to man who was holding slate.*)

Never mind the envelope, sir. Just throw it away for me, will you?

(*Holds up slate again.*)

We have all the evidence we need right here.

(*Puts slate and other things into briefcase and starts following routine.*)

Who's Worried Now?

A MAGICAL theme audiences have enjoyed for more than
a hundred years is the one in which a borrowed handkerchief is cut and then restored, after a series of amusing
misadventures in which everything seems to go wrong for
the magician. One version of this, known to magicians as the
"Sun and Moon" trick, involves a second handkerchief of a
different color, so that the cut out centers of the two become
mixed up during the by-play of making the borrowed one
whole again. It hasn't been seen as much in recent years as
it once was, perhaps because most ways of performing it
required rather expert handling of volunteer assistants, but
it is a theme that creates its own natural comedy and one
which can provide as much fun for today's audiences as it
has in the past.

In this routine, you pretend to be trying a new trick for
the first time. You cut the center from a borrowed handkerchief and also from a red bandanna handkerchief of your
own. When you put the two mutilated handkerchiefs and
the centers cut from them into a paper bag to restore them

to their original condition, the centers become mixed in the traditional way, so that the white handkerchief has a red center and the red one a white center. But in the end, everything comes out as it should, and you return the borrowed handkerchief unharmed.

There are no elaborate props or set-ups to worry about, since most of the trickery is accomplished by means of a small cardboard tube, fixed with pieces of cloth in its two ends to resemble the centers of the handkerchiefs, and by the use of a paper bag that has an extra back in which to hide things. The audience participates, but indirectly, since you need not call for volunteers to assist you, and the effect is worked right out of your briefcase, into which everything goes again when you are finished.

What you need:

Three white linen handkerchiefs. These should be men's full-sized handkerchiefs and inexpensive ones because you are going to cut two of them. The third one is not used when you actually perform the routine, but you will need it for practice.

Three red bandanna handkerchiefs.

Two flat-bottomed paper bags, the kind that will stand upright by themselves, each about about 6½″ x 12″.

All-purpose white glue.

A 3″ x 5″ office file card.

Scotch tape, scissors, and a spool of white thread.

You will need the help of someone with a sewing machine to prepare a set of handkerchiefs with mixed centers in a way that will be explained. Once these are made, they can be used whenever you perform the routine.

How you make the props:

Cut a circle 4" in diameter from the center of a red bandanna and another circle the same size from the center of a white handkerchief and put the two centers aside a moment. In another bandanna, cut a center hole 3½" in diameter, and also cut a hole 3½" in diameter in the center of a second white handkerchief. Sew the 4" piece from the center of the first bandanna to the white handkerchief that has the 3½" hole in its center by placing the red patch over the hole and double-stitching a seam around the edges. Now sew the 4" white center as a patch over the bandanna that has a 3½" hole in its center. Put those aside.

From the scraps of the first white handkerchief, cut a piece of cloth 4" square. Take it by its center, bring the ends to the bottom, and bind the ends tightly by winding white thread around them. Do the same thing with a 4" square cut from the scraps of the first bandanna.

Cut a piece 5" long and 2" wide from the file card. Form this piece into a tube 1" in diameter and glue it together. Let the glue dry thoroughly. Fasten a strip of transparent tape to the thread-tied end of the little bunch of white cloth and attach it firmly just inside the top end of the tube made from the file card. Turn the tube over and fasten the small bunch of bandanna cloth at that end in the same manner. Push the cloth pieces down inside the tube, one at each end.

Open out one of the paper bags and cut the entire back from it. Put glue along the two sides and bottom edge of this back piece and fasten it tightly to the back of the other whole bag so the tops exactly match and the extra piece looks like the back of the bag itself. This gives you a double paper bag, with a hidden pocket at the back that will let you exchange things. But since the extra piece is on the outside of the bag, you can show the inside of it quite freely.

The bag should last you quite a few shows. The only props you will have to replace each time you give a performance are the two little squares of cloth taped into the ends of the file card tube. One extra white handkerchief and one extra bandanna should provide enough material to cut squares for at least a dozen performances, so the trick will not be an expensive one to do. Fixing up the tube will take only a minute and the rest of the set-up won't take much longer.

How you use them:

Fold the prepared red bandanna diagonally and then bunch the folds so as to conceal its white center. Make as flat a bundle of it as you can and put it into the secret pocket at the rear of the bag. Fold and bunch the prepared white hand-

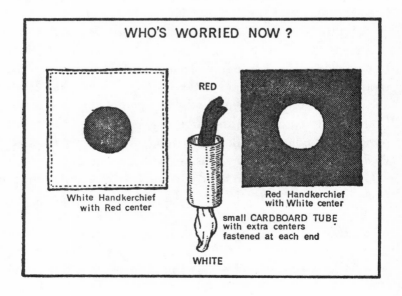

WHO'S WORRIED NOW ?

White Handkerchief
with Red center

RED

Red Handkerchief
with White center

small CARDBOARD TUBE
with extra centers
fastened at each end

WHITE

kerchief in the same way, so the folds conceal the red center, and put that into the secret pocket of the bag above the bandanna. Flatten the paper bag, fold it in half, lay the uncut bandanna on top of it, and put them in your briefcase.

Open the scissors slightly and slide one of the finger grips down into the top of the file card tube at the end containing the white cloth. Shut the scissors so the side of the tube is gripped between the two halves of the handle. This is done so that when you pick up the scissors in a natural way, the tube will come with them right into the palm of your hand. If your briefcase has an inside pocket, put the scissors into that with their points down and the tube sticking up so you can grasp the handle of the scissors easily. Otherwise rest the scissors and the tube that they clamp in the bottom of your briefcase. Everything is now set the way it will be for the show.

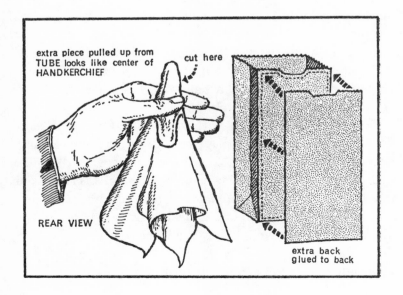

To run through the routine, you will have to use the third white handkerchief and pretend to borrow it from a man in the audience, which you will really do instead of using your own when you give the show. "Borrow" the handkerchief and hold it up by its center with your left thumb and first finger so the four ends hang down. Then close your left fingers loosely around it so the center comes inside your hand. With your right hand, take the scissors from the briefcase, holding the points up and curling your fingers naturally around the handle so they hide the little tube. Put the scissors into your left hand with the tube right against the center of the handkerchief that hand is holding. Close your left hand around the tube and the handle of the scissors.

Now bring your right hand up to the points of the scissors, which are still standing upright above your left hand. Grasp them and open them slightly as you lift the scissors up out of your left hand, leaving the tube behind. Let the scissors fall to the palm of your right hand and hold them there with the three bottom fingers of that hand. With your right first finger and thumb, reach into the top of your left fist and pull the center of the little square of cloth up out of the tube so it extends above your left hand and looks like the center of the "borrowed" handkerchief itself.

Cut off the piece of cloth with the scissors. Open it to show the center you apparently have cut out of the handkerchief. Keep your left hand as it is and put the piece on the table with your right hand. Bring your right hand back to your left and put the scissors in your left hand. Leaving the scissors there, with the tube and the handkerchief, reach into the briefcase with your right hand and take out the bandanna. Shake it open, show it, and hold it by its center with your right hand so the ends hang down.

Bring your right hand to your left and put the center of the bandanna into your left hand so its ends hang in front of the white handkerchief already there. Pull at the ends of the bandanna a little, pretending to adjust it. Now lift your right hand up until your thumb is at the bottom of the tube concealed in your left hand. Behind the covering of your two hands, as they come together for a moment, lift your thumb and turn the tube forward and upside down so the piece of bandanna is at the top of it. There is no need to make any suspicious moves. Your two hands together give the action plenty of cover and you can take your time while seeming to adjust the handkerchiefs.

Your right hand now takes the scissors from the left and your right first finger and thumb reach into the top of your left fist and pull the piece of bandanna up from the tube so it extends above your left hand and looks like the center of the bandanna itself. With the scissors, cut the piece off, open it out and show it, and then put the piece on the table next to the white piece.

Put the scissors back into your left hand. Holding your left fingers around the tube and the handle of the scissors, take away the two handkerchiefs with your right hand. Roll them together into a loose bunch so nobody can see the centers are not really cut and put them on the table. Hold up the scissors that are in your left hand as you remark that you seem to have done enough damage with them and then put them into the briefcase with that hand, leaving the tube there with them as you take out the paper bag.

Open up the bag. Hold it at the top with your right hand, fingers inside and thumb at the back, so your thumb can press against the rear compartment to keep the top of that closed. Show the bag empty and then take it at the top with your left hand. With your right hand, pick up the piece of cloth you apparently cut from the center of the "borrowed" handkerchief. Show it and put it into the rear compartment of the bag. Do this by tilting the opening of the bag toward yourself. Push your hand right down to the bottom of the hidden section, past the concealed handkerchiefs, and leave the little piece where it is well clear of them. Then pick up the circle of red bandanna. Tilt the top of the bag toward yourself once more and put that piece down into the bottom of the rear section with the other. Make sure the pieces go all the way to the bottom because it would spoil the trick if you later pulled them out by accident when you removed the concealed handkerchiefs. Now pick up the two bunched-together handkerchiefs from the table and tilt the bag the same way, but put those into the bag itself, *the front part of it, not the rear section.* Supposedly these two, the "borrowed" one and your bandanna, have their centers cut out.

Close the bag, make a "magic pass" over it, tilt the opening toward yourself, and reach into the rear section to remove the white handkerchief with the red center. Shake it out, hold it stretched between both hands to reveal what has happened, and drop it to the table. Tilt the bag so the opening is toward you, reach into the rear compartment again, and take out the red bandanna with the white center and display it.

Add the white one from the table to the one still in your hand and put first the white one and then the red one into the rear part of the bag, tilting it toward you as usual. Make another "magic pass" over the bag and then take the top of it between both hands, fingers inside and thumbs outside, and turn the bag completely upside down over the table to dump out the "borrowed" handkerchief and plain bandanna.

Holding the bag wide open, show it empty, close it and put it away in your briefcase. Pick up the bandanna from the table, open it out to show that it is restored, and then show the "borrowed" handkerchief also is undamaged.

It is a wise precaution to make sure in advance that someone has a suitable handkerchief to lend you. Speak to someone ahead of time, take him aside and explain that you will want to borrow a handkerchief during the performance. If he hasn't a plain one with him, give him yours and ask him to put it into his pocket until you request one. By doing this, you avoid any delay in borrowing a handkerchief, as well as the possibility that you may be offered one with initials or a border design that doesn't match your duplicate.

What you say and do:

MAGICIAN: I'd like to borrow . . .

(*Pauses, shakes head, smiles.*)

. . . no, not money. Just a gentleman's handkerchief. Any gentleman in the audience, please.

(*Looks to person whose handkerchief he has arranged in advance to borrow.*)

Yours, sir?

(*Hurries to take it and holds it high as he returns to table.*)

Thank you . . . this is a nice one. I almost hate to do what I am about to do.

(*Shakes it out and shows it, looks questioningly at lender.*)

This *is* the one you gave me, isn't it? I want everybody to be sure of that. You did give this one to me?

(*Smiles and starts to put handkerchief into pocket.*)

Well, since you gave it to me . . . thanks a lot.

(*Stops without actually putting it into his pocket, shakes it out again, holds it by center with left hand.*)

No ... don't worry. I'll return it to you. No worse for wear ...

(*Lowers voice slightly, as if speaking to himself.*)

... if this trick works.

(*Takes scissors from briefcase and puts them into left hand, leaving tube with them. Drops right hand to side a moment as he speaks to man who loaned handkerchief.*)

You're not worried, are you?

(*Brings up right hand, takes scissors from left, pulls what seems to be center of handkerchief from top of left fist.*)

No? Well, that's good. Because I am. This is the first time I've tried this trick. It's one I've always wanted to try ... but I never quite had the nerve.

(*Snips scissors a couple of times over top of handkerchief.*)

But what have I got to lose? It's your handkerchief.

(*Cuts piece off and opens out piece to show it.*)

I did take rather a big bite, didn't I? The whole center of it.

(*Puts cut piece on table, then looks to lender.*)

I'll tell you what I'll do ... I think it's only fair. Since this is the first time I've tried the trick, I'll invest something of mine in the risk, too.

(*Puts scissors into left hand. With right, reaches into briefcase and takes out bandanna.*)

I'll use my handkerchief as well as yours.

(*Shakes out bandanna, shows it, holds it by center and puts it with borrowed one in left hand.*)

Whatever I do to yours, I'll do to mine. Then, at least, we'll come out even.

(*Secretly reverses tube under cover of hands, takes scissors with right hand, pulls what seems to be center of ban-*)

danna out top of left fist. Cuts it off, opens up piece to show it, puts it next to white piece on table.)

Now I'll worry with you.

(*Puts scissors back into left hand, takes both handkerchiefs, bunches them loosely and puts them on table. Holds up scissors with left hand.*)

I guess I've done enough damage with these.

(*Puts scissors in briefcase, getting rid of tube with them, and takes out paper bag.*)

Since I seem to have been left holding the bag . . .

(*Makes face at poor pun, shows bag empty.*)

. . . the least I can do is gather up all the pieces so you'll have some way to carry them home.

(*Shows white piece and puts that to bottom of bag's rear section. Shows bandanna piece and puts that in. Puts the two handkerchiefs into the front part of the bag.*)

This is the part I've always wanted to try. The magic book said that if you pass your hand around the bag twice in a clockwise direction while you cast a magic spell . . .

(*Passes hand around bag, stops, looks puzzled, as if trying to remember.*)

. . . or was it counter-clockwise? I hope I don't mix this up.

(*Shrugs, looks into bag, face brightens.*)

Say, I think it worked . . . I hope.

(*Reaches into rear section, removes white handkerchief with red center, holds it outstretched to show it.*)

I guess I did get things mixed up.

(*When laughter starts to die, reaches in and takes out bandanna with white center, shows that.*)

Well, I did put them back together again. You'll have to admit that's not too bad for a first try.

(*Puts handkerchiefs back into rear section.*)

I'd better quit while fifty per cent of us are satisfied, sir.
(*Pretends to offer bag to the man.*)

I'll make a deal . . . you can have both handkerchiefs. No?
(*Lowers voice, as if talking to himself.*)

If I could only remember which way I should wave my
hand.
(*Waves it around bag one way and then the other.*)

Don't worry, sir . . . there's no point in both of us worrying.
If you'll just have the full confidence in me . . . that I wish
I had in myself—
(*Opens bag and looks in. Then, with broad smile of success, dumps bag upside down so handkerchiefs fall out to table. Shows bag empty and puts it into briefcase.*)

I'll bet you didn't really think I could do it . . . neither did I.
(*Picks up bandanna, holds it up, shows it is restored.*)

Well, mine's back together again . . . just as good as new . . .
(*Glances down at bunched white handkerchief still on table.*)

. . . and yours, sir? Why, of course it's also . . . it's . . .
(*Hesitates, lifts one corner an inch, drops it. Takes an exaggerated deep breath, whips up handkerchief and holds it open to show that it also has been restored.*)

Of course! Yes, sir . . . Of course it is! Just the way it was
when we started.
(*Takes applause and hurries down to return handkerchief.*)

Thank you.
(*Returns to table and for extra laugh strikes pose and moves arm clockwise, pauses and scratches head and frowns, then moves hand counter-clockwise, as if still can't remember which was right. Shrugs, looks at audience and smiles, and goes into next routine.*)

Let's Go to the Fair

Your closing number deliberately avoids using props to focus attention entirely on you. It is meant to impress the audience with the skill of your hands, to emphasize that the magic depends on you and not on any apparatus you might use. Actually, there is no difficult sleight of hand required, since a little push of the fingers accomplishes most of it. The plot, adapted from a card trick magicians know as "The Six Card Repeat," is a simple one. It gains both its strength and its humor from repetition. Instead of cards, small discs of thin red cardboard are used, to fit the story and give it color while still keeping the props plain so the audience will realize that only personal skill is involved.

Its theme is that during a visit to the fair, you came upon a game of chance being played with six red circles. As you tell the story, you keep throwing away some of them, but six always remain, which leads to a punch line that should end your show with laughter and a good round of applause. The magic depends on making a false count of the discs, which is not hard to learn, but must be practiced well.

What you need:

A sheet of fairly thin red cardboard large enough to cut fifteen 3½" circles from it. The cardboard must have a smooth surface so the discs will slide easily during the counting.

A compass to make the circles, or you can use the bottom of a glass or a can of approximate size.

Scissors and rubber bands.

How you make the props:

There is nothing to make, except to cut out the cardboard circles. Set the compass for the proper diameter, mark them out with it and cut them with the scissors. The discs should be close enough to being perfect circles so that you can stack them neatly. Two rubber bands are crossed around them to keep them together until you use them.

How you use them:

The false count makes use of a move magicians call "The Glide," but handled a little differently than with playing cards. Start by learning the position your hands will take for the counting. Hold your left hand a little to the left of your body, with the back of it toward the audience, fingers to the left and thumb down. Put the edge of the stack of discs against the crotch of your left thumb and close your fingers and thumb around the rear of the discs to hold them. They should extend about halfway out the bottom of your hand. Hold them easily, not with an iron-tight grip.

Now bring your right hand up under the left one so that your right thumb rests on the front bottom edge of the stack and the tips of your right fingers are at the back. With your

fingers, secretly slide the back disc of the stack about half
way up inside your left hand. The stack is now set for counting. You are going to pretend to count the fifteen discs as if
there were only six. With your right thumb, slide the top
disc down off the stack and take it away between your thumb

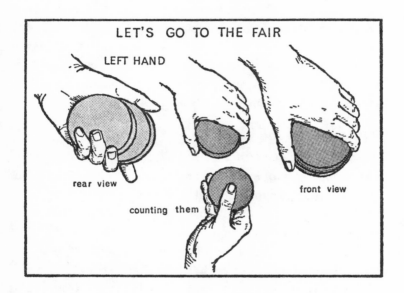

and fingers. Count off the second, third, and fourth ones the
same way, by pulling them down off the top of the stack with
your right thumb. But when you count the fifth one, take not
just one disc but the whole remaining stack of them except
for the last one, which stays for a moment in your left hand.

This is easy to do because the rear disc of the stack previously has been pushed up out of the way so you can grasp
the bottom edge of the whole stack and take them all as if
they were a single disc. Then tap the discs in your right hand
smartly against the one that remains in your left hand. Show

both sides of it with your left hand and drop it on top of the ones in your right hand. Finally, replace them all in your left hand as they were originally, so you can repeat the count again.

You need not count rapidly, but you should do it smoothly. Practice counting aloud as you take the discs one at a time with your right hand until you can make the false count with an unbroken rhythm. It should look as if you are doing nothing but counting six discs from one hand to the other. To set things up for the show, just put the rubber bands around the stack and put them into your briefcase.

What you say and do:

MAGICIAN: (*Takes stack of red discs from briefcase as he speaks, removes rubber bands, and tosses bands away.*) I was out at the fair grounds recently, out where they have all those games you bet on ... the numbered wheels that spin around, the stuffed cats you knock over with baseballs, the saucers you try to pitch pennies into ... but there was one fellow who had a game I hadn't ever seen before. He had a table in front of him and a crowd was gathered around and he was taking bets on some little red circles he had in his hand. He kept moving them so you began to feel you were seeing spots before your eyes. It went something like this ...

(*Imitates loud, glib monotone and brash, breezy manner of a carnival man addressing a crowd at a fair.*)

Step right up, folks! Step right in a little closer! I'm going to show you the easiest way on the midway to make yourselves a little money. All you have to do is watch the little red spots and bet on how many of them I have in my hand ... and I'm going to count them for you.

(*Puts stack of fifteen in left hand and counts aloud, making false count as practiced.*)

I have one, two, three, four, five . . . and six.

(*Puts stack back in left hand as before.*)

Now I'm going to throw away three of these . . .

(*Takes three off top of stack, one at a time, throwing each to the table as he counts.*)

. . . one . . . . two . . . three. It's the red that gets you, folks. It's what the per-fessors call psychological.

(*With right hand, slaps the remainder of the stack in his left hand.*)

How many have I got? How many have I got? Put up your money, folks! Put up your bets!

(*Carnival man pretends to hear someone in crowd answer.*)

What'd you say, m'am? You said I have three? I'm sorry . . . I told you I had six.

(*Counts them aloud, making false count on fifth to take all but one as a single disc, as before.*)

One, two, three, four, five . . . and six. Now I'm going to throw away . . .

(*Counts off three, throwing each to table as he pulls them off stack.*)

. . . one, two, three.

(*Slaps remainder of stack with right hand.*)

How many have I got? How many have I left? Put up your money, folks! Put up your bets! . . . What'd you say, bud? Three? I'm sorry . . . sorry. I told you I had six.

(*Makes false count again.*)

One, two, three, four, five . . . and six.

(*Not imitating carnival man now, magician speaks more quietly, in his own voice, as if going on with story of his visit to the fair. Makes gesture of picking up money from table and putting it into his pocket.*)

He picked up the money and put it in his pocket ... well, I waited until the crowd went away and then I went over to him. I told him it was a good trick. I said I was a magician and maybe we could swap a few ideas ... I'd show him some of my tricks if he would show me how he worked the one with the little red spots. He said ...

(*Imitates carnival man's voice.*)

... you're on, bud. You're a live one ... Sure, I always like to learn new tricks.

(*Speaks in own voice again.*)

So I showed him a few tricks of mine and he seemed to like them. But then he started to walk away. I stopped him and said ... hey, you were going to show me that one of yours with the red spots, remember? He said ...

(*Imitates carnival man's voice.*)

... Sure, bud, sure. I'll show you exactly how it goes. First ... you put your money down right here.

(*Points to table.*)

Then you count the little red spots.

(*Puts stack in left hand, makes false count.*)

I have one, two, three, four, five ... and six. Now here's the tricky part, bud, the tricky part ... so watch me closely. I'm going to throw away three of these.

(*Counts them off, throwing each on table as he counts.*)

One, two, three.

(*Slaps right hand against remaining stack.*)

How many have I left? How many have I left?

(*Magician speaks in own voice.*)

Well, I thought a minute and I said ... three from six leaves ...

(*Frowns and counts on fingers, holding up right hand to tap tips of them with index finger of left.*)

... one, two ... (*Uncertainly*) ... three? He said ...

(*Imitates carnival man.*)

... I'm sorry, bud, sorry. I told you I had ...

(*Counts them, letting each one fall singly from hand to table to emphasize count.*)

... one ... two ... three ... four ... five ... and six.

(*Magician speaks quickly in own voice again.*)

And he picked up my money ... (*Pretends to.*) ... and put it in his pocket and walked off and ...

(*Smiles sadly and shakes head.*)

... I never *did* learn *how* that trick was done.

(*After laughter and applause, bows, lifts hands in gesture of thanks.*)

Thank you. This has been fun for me and I hope it has been for you ... Good night.

The briefcase set-up

You will find it a lot easier to handle the props without delay during your performance if you use a briefcase with a center partition that divides it. Set up everything in the half that will be the bottom of the briefcase when it rests flat on your table during the show. Then, as you finish a routine, put the props that have been used in the top part of the briefcase, so the partition will keep them from becoming mixed with things not yet shown. If your briefcase has no partition, you can make a serviceable one with a piece of stiff cardboard cut to fit into it.

It is a good rule to make a habit of setting things up in your briefcase for another show as soon as you get home from one you have given. If the tricks are ones you will do regularly, make up a supply of the props that have to be replaced. Keep the extras on a shelf in separate cardboard boxes, marked on their fronts so you can tell at a glance what is in each of them. Then it is a simple matter to put everything together for another show, so you will always have your briefcase ready and can just pick it up and go whenever you're invited to entertain.

ACT FOUR

For the Kids

THIS is a show planned for an audience of young children, boys and girls mostly under the age of nine, the kind of a performance that magicians call a "kid show." It is an entertainment you might give at a children's party sponsored by some club or church, at a birthday party in a child's home, or for a junior group at school or camp. This sort of a show requires an approach entirely different from that of any other. The magic becomes a game that you and your young audience play together, and the props become not puzzles to confuse, but delightful surprises that are part of the pretending.

Young children also are far less sure of themselves than those even a few years older. While they love the surprise of magic and the fun of it that leads to unexpected happenings, they hate to be fooled in any way that makes them appear stupid. That is why the magician has to be very careful to avoid assuming a superior attitude or any hint that he

155

is smarter than they are because he's a little older and they are "just kids."

Even when they don't know the real explanation of a trick, some are almost sure to shout, "Aw, I know how that's done," or, "It went up his sleeve!" A certain amount of such shouting is part of the fun and the wise magician ignores it and goes on with his show. He never directly answers such a taunt or tries to argue about it. His best answer is to show something else that is so interesting the shouts will die because his viewers don't want to miss what is coming next.

Above all, he should practice his show so well that he knows exactly what he is doing and what he intends to do next. If he is friendly and sure of himself, and moves smoothly from one thing to the next, the game is not likely to turn into one of taunts. He should plan the show so there is plenty of opportunity for vocal response, but at times that he chooses.

The first impression he makes on a very young audience is more vital than in any other kind of a magic show. He must put across the idea that it is all for fun. As he goes on into his tricks, he should keep stressing that. The by-play and clowning that grow out of the routines can be more entertaining than the magic itself. The tricks must be simple and direct in plot, clearly understood and easy to follow.

Young boys and girls are anxious to get up and help the magician and they should be given that chance as often as possible. But the same rules hold as when choosing volunteer assistants from an audience of older persons. Don't make a vague and general request for a helper. Select some one youngster and go to him directly, or point to him. Say, "Will the young man in the blue sweater, right there in the front row, help me with this?"

If you are on a platform, go to the steps and help lead him up to make sure his eagerness doesn't cause him to trip and fall. When he gets there, ask him his name. Introduce yourself and call him by name. After you have finished the trick, shake his hand, thank him by name, and see to it that he gets safely back to his seat. Remember, too, that the very young often have difficulty following instructions. Don't give him anything too hard to do.

It adds to the fun if you have some "magic words" to use. Make up a phrase connected with the particular show you are giving. If it is a cub scout show, the words might be: "Cub Pack Fourteen." For a birthday party, you might use the name of the boy or girl whose birthday it is. Explain to the group that you want them to learn the "magic words" so they can shout them together. Have them try it a few times. Then when you come to the part of any trick where you are about to make the magic happen, give your signal and let them shout. This not only gives a reason for the magic, but also makes them feel that they have more of a part in it.

Where's the Wand?

Y<small>OU</small> start your show with a little verbal by-play that makes friends with the audience and also sets the tone that this is to be entirely for fun. Since there is nothing more magical to most young minds than a magic wand, you then produce one. But it is a tiny wand that they can hardly see. So your first quick magic is to stretch it to normal size. You put the tiny wand into a purse and it grows big.

Then you make the magic a game for everybody by getting a boy from the audience to help you and having him hold the wand in a bit of clowning in which he is going to make the whole audience "vanish out of sight." Instead, he vanishes the wand itself from a sheet of newspaper and, after congratulating him on having done a better trick than you could do, you help him hunt for the missing wand. The shouts of the audience finally help you find it, hanging to the boy's back.

The trick is one of the few that really does make use of your sleeve, for that is where the big wand is hidden, waiting to be pulled through a secret slit in the side of a small clasp purse where you have put the tiny wand from which the big one seems to grow. The second part of the trick employs a hook attached to one tip of the wand so it can be hooked to the boy's back while the audience thinks it is still wrapped in the paper he holds. They are convinced it is in the paper until the very last minute because you rap the paper on the table to prove the wand is there. The sound really comes from a small lead weight, used in the way that one was used in the *No Soap* trick.

This and several of the other routines to follow have been planned to include some of the props already explained, so you can see how the secrets of one trick may be changed to use for another. In making up routines of your own, you will discover that one basic idea such as this can lead to many new effects. Other uses for some of these props are suggested in the last part of the book, under the heading, *Building Your Own Routines.*

What you need:

A small clasp-type coin purse.
A "kitchen" match.
A 12" piece of ½" wooden dowel rod.
White plastic adhesive tape 1½" wide.
One straight pin.
A piece of newspaper 7"x 14".
A small lead fishing sinker (size 3.)
Black enamel paint and a brush.
Scotch tape and a razor blade in a holder.

How you make the props:

Open the purse and, with the razor blade, make a horizontal 2" long slit across one side, about 1" up from the bottom.

Turn the piece of newspaper so its short edges are top and bottom. With the Scotch tape, fasten the lead sinker about 2″ from the bottom of the paper and the same distance in from the left edge. Roll the paper into a long tube which has a diameter of about ¾″. Put horizontal strips of transparent tape near the top, center and bottom to keep the tube from unrolling. Fold up the bottom of the tube right at the point where the lead sinker is inside it. Fasten the folded part to the side of the tube with a strip of transparent tape.

Now to make the big wand and the little one, start by painting the dowel rod and the match with black enamel and let them dry. Cut two short strips of the white plastic adhesive tape ¼″ wide. Band one around each end of the match and you have the tiny wand. Next cut a piece of the white plastic tape 1″ long. Take the painted dowel rod, hold it upright, and place the head of the pin at one edge so the pin lies across the center of the top of the rod. Bend the point of the pin down until it almost, but not quite, touches the side of the stick. Hold it that way with your left index finger on top of it. With your right hand, take the piece of tape that you cut and bring it up so that the point of the pin goes through the tape. Draw the tape back across the top of the rod, press it firmly in place so as to hold the pin there, and then smooth the tape to the sides of the stick.

Cut a piece of the tape 2″ long, bring it up under the pin, and wrap it neatly and horizontally around the rod at that end. Place a 1″ long piece of tape over the other end and then wrap a 2″ strip around the end. The result should be a black wand with two white tips, at one end of which there is a small pointed hook formed by the bent pin. Finally cut another piece of tape ¼″ wide and 1″ long and wrap that over the top part of the hook and around the wand. It helps to shorten the exposed part of the hook and also to hold it more firmly.

How you use them:

Drop the tiny wand into the purse. Put the hook end of the big wand up through the slit in the side of the purse, snap the purse shut, and then tilt the other end of the wand as far to the left as the slit will let it go. Put on your jacket and slide the end of the wand up your left sleeve. Rest the bottom of the purse on the palm of your left hand, close your thumb and fingers loosely, and drop your left arm to your side so it hangs there naturally.

If you are performing where there are curtains, you will enter holding the purse this way. Where there are no curtains, you will keep the purse, with the wand fixed through the slit of it, in your suitcase. Just before you start the show, slide the wand up your sleeve, using the lid of the suitcase

WHERE'S THE WAND ?

HOOK WAND

HOOK IS OVER EDGE OF NEWS— PAPER TUBE

LEAD WEIGHT IS WHERE TUBE IS FOLDED UP AT END

EMPTY TUBE SOUNDS LIKE WAND WHEN WEIGHT TAPS TABLE

as a screen to keep anyone out front from seeing what you are doing.

With the wand and purse in position, hold your left hand chest-high in front of you. Open the purse with your right hand, take out the tiny wand and show it, and drop it back into the purse. Shut the purse. Snap your fingers, reach in again, and pull the big one up and out. The wand seems to have grown in size.

That's the first part of the routine. To try the second part, you can hang your jacket on the back of a chair and pretend it is one a boy from the audience is wearing. Put the chair a few feet to the right of your table and a little to the rear of it, which is where you will have him stand. Have the paper tube on the table. You will stand behind the table, to the boy's left.

Hold the wand loosely with your right hand around the hook end and rap the other end twice on the table. With your left hand, hold the tube upright and slide the wand down into it so that the hook catches over the edge of the paper at the top. Close your right hand around that top end of the tube and take the tube from your left hand. With your right hand, rap the tube twice on the table, but do it so the flattened end with the lead weight strikes the table top and actually makes the sound.

For a moment, you will be talking and holding the wand that way. You then place your left hand on the boy's shoulder and your right hand on his back, to move him back a little. As your right hand goes behind him, catch the hook at the center of his shoulders, gently pull the paper tube straight down, and the wand will remain hooked to his back. But you immediately step away, holding the paper tube, and the audience has no reason to suspect the wand is not still in it. In fact, they are certain a moment later when the routine gives you good reason to rap the weighted end of the tube on the table so it sounds like the wand.

Folding the open end of the tube shut, you have the boy hold the tube by both ends. He finally tears open the paper to reveal that the wand has vanished. You take his hand and walk around with him, looking for it. At first you ignore the shouts from the audience that it is hanging on his back, but the two of you finally discover it there, much to your own pretended surprise.

Use the jacket over the back of the chair for practice and you will find that just a touch of the wand hooks it on so you easily can pull the tube free. Try it before the mirror until the action looks entirely natural, seeming as if you just helped him to move back a step. When you choose your helper from the audience, try to find a boy wearing a sweater if not a jacket. However, the hook is so tiny that even if he is wearing only a shirt, he isn't likely to feel it. Anyhow, you're going to keep him too busy to notice.

What you say and do:

MAGICIAN: (*Left hand hangs naturally at side with wand-loaded purse loosely held in hand. Walks briskly and confidently forward, smiles and speaks.*) Hello . . . my name is Bill Smith. (*Uses own name.*) Let's introduce ourselves. When I ask what your names are, I want you all to call them out. All at once, okay? I'll start again . . .

(*Backs a few steps, comes forward as before, smiles.*)

My name is Bill Smith. (*Uses own name.*) What's yours?

(*As they shout, he cups right hand to ear.*)

I'm sorry . . . I didn't hear you. What did you say your name was?

(*They shout again. He smiles.*)

Good . . . now that we're all acquainted and good friends, let's have some fun together with magic. I want to show you my bag of tricks.

(*Left hand holds up purse.*)

Well, it *was* my bag of tricks . . . until I left it out in the rain. It was as big as that other bag over there . . .

(*Right hand points to suitcase on chair.*)

. . . but it shrank.

(*Right hand opens purse and takes out tiny wand and he shakes his head over it. Puts wand back into purse as finishes speaking, shuts it.*)

Look what happened to my poor magic wand. With such a tiny wand, I can do only little tricks. But maybe you can help me. There are some magic words you can say. We'll learn them together and then when I snap my fingers, everybody say them, and if you shout them loudly enough, maybe the magic will work. The magic words are . . .

(*He gives them, localizing so they apply to that show.*)

Want to try it? When I snap my fingers, everybody say the magic words . . . are you ready?

(*Snaps fingers. They shout.*)

Thank you . . . you see, you did make it work . . . you made the wand grow up.

(*Opens purse, pulls out big wand, puts purse in left jacket pocket.*)

Remember those words . . . we may need them again. Since you've all been such good friends, helping me out like that with my magic, I'm going to make . . .

(*Goes to boy he wants as a helper or points to him directly with wand.*)

... that young man right there, the one with a green sweater, into a magician ... Would you like to be a magician?

(*Brings him up.*)

You know, I just heard your name when you all called them out, but there were so many all at once, maybe you'd better tell me again ... what is your name? George (*Uses boy's name.*) Of course, George ... that's right. I'm glad to meet you again, George. (*Shakes hand.*) As long as we have a big wand now, we might as well start off with a big trick. You are about to make the whole audience disappear from sight ... make them vanish from before your very eyes. Do you think you can do that, George?

(*Whatever he says, continues.*)

Well, I'm sure you can. But you know, I think ... until you get the hang of it ... we'd better reduce the power of this wand a little. (*Raps wand on table.*) Otherwise you might make the whole city disappear from sight. We'll put some paper over it to dim it some.

(*Slides wand into tube. Raps weighted paper on table to accustom audience to sound.*)

Now let's line things up, George.

(*Holds wand in front of him and pretends to sight along it to measure distance.*)

I think you'd better step back just a little ...

(*Puts left hand on boy's shoulder, right hand at his back, leaves wand hanging on boy's back. Holds up empty tube as if wand were still in it and sights along it again.*)

... that's fine. Exactly right. Don't move. Are you ready to make the audience vanish from sight?

(*Closes other end of paper tube.*)

When I rap the wand twice on the table, I want you to shut your eyes tight . . . and don't open them until I say. All right?

(*Raps weighted paper twice on table.*)

Can you see the audience with your eyes shut? No? Then they *have* disappeared from your sight . . . just as I said they would. The whole audience has vanished from before your eyes. But I'll bring them back again.

(*Raps tube on table.*)

Open your eyes . . . there they are! (*Smiles.*) There wasn't much magic in that, was there? Maybe you'd rather try some magic with your eyes wide open . . . Hold your two hands up, George. Take one end of the wand in this hand . . . and the other end of it in this.

(*Puts one end of tube in each of boy's hands so it is held horizontally between them.*)

Now lift your hands up very slowly . . . while we all say the magic words.

(*Looks to audience and snaps fingers. They shout the magic words. Turns to boy.*)

What happened? Nothing? That's strange . . . You know, I think we dimmed the wand too much. Too much paper around it so it hasn't enough power left. George, why don't you tear the paper right at the middle . . . take off half of it so we can make the wand—

(*If boy tears paper, magician steps back, looks startled over disappearance of wand. If boy has trouble tearing paper, he himself tears tube in half.*)

Something certainly did happen! Where's the wand?

(*Takes torn tube. Tears it to pieces, crumples it, looks up at ceiling, down at floor, as if searching for wand.*)

Reverse magic . . . that's what happened! The wand itself

disappeared . . . That's some trick, George. Better than I could do.

(*Puts hand on boy's shoulder to keep him from turning. Looks to audience.*)

Let's all give him a hand. You're quite a magician.

(*Leads applause. Speaks again when it quiets.*)

But how can we go on with the show without a wand? Will you help me try to find it?

(*Takes boy's hand and leads him forward. Turns him so they walk back together. Audience shouts that it is on boy's back.*)

Back? . . . back where?

(*Looks to audience, then to boy.*)

They say it's back here somewhere . . . I don't see it, do you?

(*Shouting grows louder.*)

I think they're trying to tell us something. I think . . .

(*Sees it on boy's back. Steps away laughing. Removes wand and holds it up.*)

How in the world did you do that? . . . Thank you, George.

(*Shakes his hand, leads him back to seat.*)

He certainly is a good magician.

(*Claps own hands to lead applause for boy. Puts wand on table. Picks up jump rope.*)

Jump for Joy

HAVING had a boy help you, you now get a little girl to join you in a magical game of jumping rope. You give her a jump rope and let her try using it, while the audience applauds her efforts. Then you tell her that you know a much easier way to jump rope and ask to borrow the rope for a minute. You hold it as if you were going to jump it, which gives you a chance for a little clowning. Taking a pair of scissors from your pocket, you cut the rope in half, explaining that it makes the jumping a lot easier because your feet won't get caught in the rope.

Holding a piece in each hand, you pretend to jump rope with them. Finally you offer to give the girl the rope and you put the two pieces in a paper bag for her to carry home. But you wouldn't really give her such a poor present, a jump rope that had been ruined by cutting it in two, so everybody shouts the "magic words" and you rip the bag wide open to reveal that the rope has been made whole again. You then give her the magic jump rope to keep.

The paper bag accomplishes the trick. It is a large party "loot bag," made in such a way as to pull wide open in an instant and show that it apparently is empty. But it has an extra back, similar to the bag used in *Who's Worried Now?* The cut pieces are dropped into the hidden part to exchange them for the whole rope which was in the bag at the start.

If your audience happens to be all boys, instead of a mixed one that includes girls, you still can use the routine. Simply change the start of the story a little by making a remark or two about boxers and other athletes who use jump ropes in training. If none of the boys present knows how to jump rope, you offer to show how to do it and go on with the effect from there.

What you need:

Two inexpensive jump ropes with wooden handles. You will give away one of these each time you perform. Each should be about two yards long and they should be exact duplicates.

A sharp pair of scissors that will fit into your breast pocket.

Double-stick transparent tape, the kind sticky on both sides.

White all-purpose glue.

A supply of "loot bags." These are sold in some variety stores and gift shops with the words "loot bag" printed on them and are familiar to party-going youngsters who use them to carry home their goodies. But any brightly decorated and sturdy colored paper bags, about 12" x 15" in size, may be used as long as they cannot be seen through easily. You will need two to make up the trick bag and a third one to give the girl who helps you when you present her with the restored jump rope.

How you make the props:

While the bag is prepared in somewhat the same way as the double-backed one previously used in *Who's Worried Now?*, it is also fixed so it can be ripped wide open quickly to reveal the entire inside. Once made, it should last you for several shows.

Use a blade of the scissors, or a letter opener if you prefer, to slit one of the bags down the entire length of its two sides so as to open it out flat. Trim both sides neatly to remove any paper fuzz. Put a vertical 2″ long strip of double-stick tape about 1″ down from the top left corner of what was the inside back of the bag. On the same side, about 3″ below the first one, fasten another vertical strip of tape the same length. Three inches below that, put still another. Now put matching 2″ strips of the double-stick tape down the right side. Close up the bag so the edges neatly match and press where the tapes are so as to stick the bag firmly back together.

Turn the bag face down on a table. Cut the entire back from a second bag. Coat both the side edges and the bottom edge with all-purpose glue. Turn the piece over and glue it to the back of the first bag so that all the edges match and it looks like the back of the bag itself.

How you use them:

Put a plain unprepared bag on the table. Fold up one of the jump ropes so it makes a neat bundle about 10″ long and place it in the bottom of the front part of the trick bag. Put that bag on top of the other. Have the second jump rope next to the bags and the scissors, points down, in your breast pocket. That is how things will be set for the show.

To run through the magic itself, without any of the clowning that is part of the routine, pretend for now that the jump rope has been cut in half. You have held a piece of it in each hand and gathered both in your right hand. Pick up the bag with your left hand at the bottom, tilt it back so the mouth of it is toward you, and put the halves of rope into the secret back pocket.

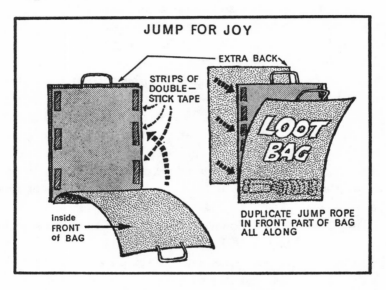

JUMP FOR JOY

EXTRA BACK

STRIPS OF DOUBLE—STICK TAPE

LOOT BAG

inside FRONT of BAG

DUPLICATE JUMP ROPE IN FRONT PART OF BAG ALL ALONG

Now transfer the bag to your right hand, taking it at the top back edge with your fingers inside and your thumb outside. The front of the bag should face the audience. Bring your left hand to the top and close your fingers over the top front edge. Pull straight down with your left hand and the bag will rip wide open as the strips of tape pull free. This shoots the rope into the air so it falls to the floor. Take your left hand away from the bag. With your right hand, turn it to show both sides, fold it together again and put it in your suitcase. Pick up the duplicate whole rope from the floor, tug it between both hands to prove the pieces really have come together, and then take the second bag from the table, drop the rope into it and present it to the girl as a magic jump rope to take home with her.

After you have used the bag a few times, you will have to replace the strips of double-stick tape to make sure it doesn't come open prematurely. But don't try to tear off the old strips. Just put new ones right over them.

What you say and do:

MAGICIAN: (*Picks up jump rope from table and displays it by holding a handle in each hand.*) Hold up your hands . . . how many of you can jump rope?

(*From those with hands up, he mentally chooses the most likely girl helper. Goes to her and gives her the rope or, if on a platform, points to her with the handle of it.*)

The young lady right there . . . with the pink dress. Will you jump rope with me?

(*Leads her up, asks her name, introduces himself, has her try the jump rope by jumping with it a few times.*)

Say, that's good!

(*Leads applause for her.*)

Do you know any rhymes to go with it? I remember one we used to say:

> Pick up a penny and pick up a pin,
> Jump right out and jump right in!

(*Gets her to jump while he repeats the rhyme for her, or some other simple jumping rhyme, and leads applause again when she finishes. But if she can't jump well, he goes on with routine without having her jump a second time.*)

I know a way that makes jumping much easier. Will you let me show you? May I borrow the rope a minute, Joan? (*Uses her name.*) My trouble is that my feet always get tangled up in it.

(*Takes rope by handles as if going to jump with it. Swings it behind him. Takes deep breath, hesitates, swings it forward, but doesn't jump.*)

It is hard, isn't it? But here's the way I figured out to make it easier.

(*Takes rope at center, removes scissors, cuts rope in two. Puts scissors back into pocket. Takes one half of rope by handle in each hand and swings them around as if jumping.*)

See how much easier that is? You don't trip over the rope.

(*Smiles at audience.*)

Well, I didn't say it was better . . . just that it was easier . . . I'll make you a present of this jump rope, Joan.

(*Holds up the two halves and looks from one to the other.*)

It's almost as good as new. All you have to do is paste it together in the middle. I'll put it in a bag for you, so you can carry it home.

(*Picks up loot bag, tilts it, puts cut pieces in hidden pocket. Frowns as if troubled.*)

Maybe you could pin it together. That might be better than paste . . . or get the dog to chew on the ends of it and then when they're all stringy, you can braid them together . . . or maybe—

(*Halts and smiles as if he had an inspiration.*)

I wonder if the magic words will work?

(*Looks out at audience.*)

When I give you the signal, let's all shout them and see.

(*Snaps fingers, shouts with them, rips bag wide open so rope shoots up into air and lands on floor. Quickly shows both sides of bag, closes it and drops it into suitcase on chair. Picks up rope from floor, tests it between hands, then coils it up as he speaks.)*

You didn't really think I'd give you that kind of a present, did you, Joan? An old cut-up piece of rope? What's the use in being a magician if you can't do something about things like that? I'll get a fresh bag for you to carry it home.

(Drops rope into bag and gives it to girl.)

There you are, Joan. A magic jump rope for you. Thank you very much for helping me.

(Leads applause for her.)

Let's give her a hand.

(Sees that she safely returns to her seat. Turns to audience.)

And thank you all, too ... for saying the magic words. How would you like to go on an Indian hunting trip with me? Well, that's what we're going to do next.

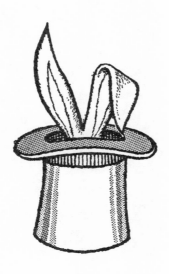

The Magic Arrow

SEVERAL boys and girls take part in your next routine, but to keep things moving smoothly and to avoid difficulties in handling a group, only one boy leaves his seat to help you. The routine really is a card trick, but since an audience as young as yours might have trouble identifying playing cards by name and very likely would be bored anyhow if you were to present "just a card trick," which is something their older brothers can do, you dress it up. You avoid mentioning "cards" as you show some "pictures."

These are cards with pictures representing various letters of the alphabet, such as an apple for the letter "A," a barn for the letter "B," a picture of a tree for the letter "T," and so on. You hand out batches of them to four or five boys and girls. Then you have one of the pictures chosen and mixed in its pile with the others. A boy helps by taking a paper bag, making sure it is empty, and collecting all the pictures in it. Each youngster who is holding some of them is asked, not to "shuffle the cards," but to "mix up the pictures," and the boy with the bag also mixes them each time a batch is dropped in. He finally brings the bag to you.

You show an arrow and after telling a story about it, thrust it right through the paper bag from back to front. Holding the arrow, you rip away the paper bag. The chosen picture is impaled on the arrow. The arrow magically has found its target by landing in the card that pictures the tree. A duplicate card and a little strip of double-stick tape accomplishes the trickery.

What you need:

A paper bag, about 5″ x 11″, with a flat bottom so it will stand up by itself.

A white pocket handkerchief.

An arrow about 24″ long, with a metal tip.

Double-stick transparent tape, the kind sticky on both sides.

A small metal tray, about 9″ x 14″.

Two identical packs of alphabet picture cards, about the size of playing cards. These come in many varieties. Try to find packs with large pictures, one of which is a picture of a tree for the letter "T." You may, of course, use a different card, by changing the story a little, or choose cards that picture something else rather than letters of the alphabet. But the pictures should be simple ones that are easy to identify. Since an arrow is to go through one of them, you will want to avoid cards that picture either people or animals.

How you make the props:

Make a hole in one of the "tree" cards by working the tip of the arrow right through the center of it from front to back. Remove the arrow and press the punctured part flat again with your fingers so that the surface of the card is reasonably smooth. The hole is not going to be hidden, but if the rough edges stick up they may interfere with the smooth working

of the trick. Now turn this card face down and put two strips
of double-stick tape horizontally across its back, one a little
above and the other a little below the hole you have made.
By replacing the sticky tape when necessary, the card may be
used many times.

How you use them:

Turn the tray so one of its short edges is toward the audience. Put the prepared card face down near the back of the
tray. Stand the opened paper bag at the front of the tray.
Now if you "accidentally" tip the bag backwards, so that it
lands on its rear side, and then press down on the bag in the
act of straightening it so that it will stand up by itself at
the front of the tray again, you will find that the taped card
has become stuck to the back of it. This is the main secret
of the trick.

When performing it, you will push the arrow from the rear
right through the hole in the card and on through the bag
itself until it comes about 8″ out the front side of the bag.
By holding the arrow and tearing the bag down off it, to rip
it away, you reveal the chosen picture card impaled on the
arrow, as if it had gone through one of the cards that were
mixed up inside the bag.

You will "accidentally" tip the bag over when picking up
the arrow to show it. Try this by putting the prepared card
near the back of the tray and an upright bag at the front of
the tray with the cards inside it. Rest the arrow across the
edge of the tray in front of the bag. Stand to the left of the
table and pick up the arrow with your right hand. Bring it
upward against the face of the bag and then just push the
bag over with it until it rests with its rear side on the card.
Press down on the bag firmly with your left hand as you
reach to set it upright again. You may find you have to pick

up the bag and shake it a little so the cards inside it will fall flat and the bag will stand up by itself.

There is no reason for haste in making this move. Don't swat the bag with the arrow or try to knock it over by slapping it backwards. Use the side of the arrow to push it over and then "carry through" the stroke by bringing the arrow on back past the tray. With a little practice, you will be able to do this without looking at the bag directly. Then look, "discover" that the bag has been tipped over, and take your time pressing upon it with your other hand as you right the bag again.

A duplicate of the card has to be the one chosen. While magicians know many extremely clever ways of forcing the choice of cards, there is no need for clever methods here. Anything that involves tricky moves or handling the cards as they might be handled for a card trick should be avoided. You simply have the duplicate of the tree card on top of the

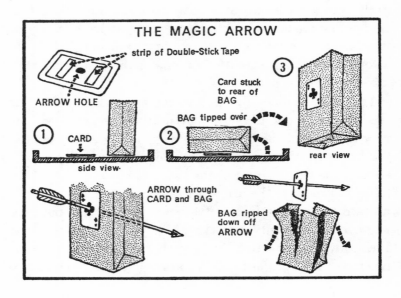

THE MAGIC ARROW

pack and take some of the cards, including that one, from the top and hand them to a boy or girl. Then you ask if you may have one of the cards and immediately reach for the top one and take it.

"Which one did you decide to give me?" you ask, looking at it and then holding it up for all to see. "The one with the picture of a tree. The letter 'T' for tree. Will somebody please remember that?" You then give it back and ask to have it mixed in well, so it is lost among the others. Later on, you ask, "Which one was it you chose to give me? I don't remember." You have planted the idea that any of the cards might have been chosen.

To set things up for the routine, place the taped card face down near the back of the tray. Open the pocket handkerchief and drop it over the card. The bag and the edge of the tray itself will hide the card from the view of the audience, but covering it with the handkerchief provides extra concealment so that young helpers you have up for earlier tricks, or anyone happening to glance at the tray just before the show, will not see the card there. But put the handkerchief over it lightly so the taped card doesn't stick to it.

Put the deck of picture cards, with the duplicate of the prepared one on top, in the paper bag. Rest the bag upright at the front of the tray. Lay the arrow across the edge in front of the bag and you are ready to perform.

What you say and do:

MAGICIAN: (*Takes picture cards from bag and steps forward with them.*) I have some pictures here that stand for different letters of the alphabet. But don't worry... (*Smiles.*) ... we're not going to have a spelling lesson or anything like that. School's out ... we'll just have some fun. There are a lot of different pictures.

(*Holds up pack, removes a few from the face of it, naming them and putting them back on the face, without disturbing those on top.*)

There's "A" for apple, "B" for barn, "C" for cat, "D" for dog . . . pictures of things for all the letters.

(*Goes to boy down front.*)

Will you take some?

(*Hands him a small batch of cards from the top, but doesn't release his own fingers from them until he finishes giving the boy directions. Helps boy grasp them.*)

Just hold them tightly like this and lift them up over your head so everybody can see them. Keep them up there now.

(*He thus prevents boy from accidentally mixing cards.*)

And will you have some of the pictures?

(*Hands a small batch to another boy or girl.*)

Hold yours up, too . . . and here are some for you to hold . . . and some for you . . . and for you. . . and how about you, over here?

(*Continues handing out batches of cards quickly, having each boy or girl hold them above head. Returns to first boy.*)

You can take your hand down now. Everybody's seen them . . . will you give me one of your pictures for a minute?

(*As he speaks, he reaches and takes the top one from those the boy is holding.*)

Which one did you decide to give me?

(*Looks at it and shows it to audience.*)

The picture of a tree. "T" is for tree. Will somebody remember that, in case I forget it?

(*Hands it back.*)

Now will you mix that one with the others you have . . . put some of them on top and some on bottom . . . mix them all up so the tree gets lost.

(*Looks along row to other boys and girls who have cards.*)

And the rest of you . . . mix yours up, too.

(*Goes to table and picks up paper bag. Watches the mixing a moment.*)

Oh, you can do better than that . . . really mix them up so they all get lost and nobody can tell what picture is where.

(*Calls up a boy he has decided to choose as his helper, one who is not among those holding cards, introduces himself, shakes his hand, and thereafter calls the boy by his name.*)

I want you to take this paper bag, Fred.

(*Holds it for him to look inside.*)

What's in there? . . . Nothing, that's right. But you'd better be sure. No purple elephants hiding in the bottom? Take a good look.

(*Turns to audience.*)

Don't stop mixing . . .

(*Gives bag to boy.*)

. . . I want you to do some mixing, too, Fred. Take the bag down and collect all the pictures from each of our friends. As each one drops them in . . . you mix them up some more.

(*Leads him to first boy with cards.*)

That's right . . . just drop yours into the bag Fred has.

(*Addresses boy with bag.*)

And you put your hand in and mix them. Upside down, stir them up, mix them any way you like.

(*Watches him collect first batches to make sure cards are returned and to hurry it along.*)

Now his pictures and hers . . . mix those with the others.

(*Returns to table.*)

When you have them all, bring the bag up here, Fred . . . if that arm is getting tired of mixing, use the other one a while.

(*When boy brings bag, takes it from him, shakes his hand, and then sees that he gets back to his seat.*)

You're a good mixer, Fred . . . the rest of you, too. If I ever want to get things mixed up, I'll know just where to go.

(*Puts hand over top of bag, vigorously shakes cards himself, turning bag upside down, and then looks into top of it.*)

I guess that's enough. They're so mixed up now, I could never straighten them out. Thank goodness, I don't have to.

(*Rests bag at front of tray. Picks up handkerchief with one hand, arrow with other, and polishes tip of arrow with handkerchief as he speaks, finally tossing handkerchief on table away from tray and replacing arrow across front edge of tray where it was.*)

How many of you know the poem *Hiawatha?* Let's see your hands? (*Nods.*) Then you all know what a wonderful hunter he was with his bow and arrow. But I'll bet you didn't know that Hiawatha used a magic arrow . . . well, I didn't either. (*Smiles.*) I just made that up. But it would have helped even Hiawatha if he'd had a magic arrow. Because with a magic arrow, you always hit the target . . . unless you happen to miss.

(*Picks up arrow again, "accidentally" tipping over bag, then straightening it in way practiced, so card secretly sticks to back of it.*)

With a magic arrow, you have to be very careful that it doesn't get a speck of dust on it.

(*Takes handkerchief, wipes tip once more, discards handkerchief.*)

Even one tiny speck of dust would weigh it down so it wouldn't fly right at all.

(*Pretends to pick speck from tip of it, throws imaginary speck to floor, looks down and slaps foot down hard on it.*)

That one was moving . . . probably a mosquito trying to get a free ride.

(*Picks up bag, holds it up, puts it back on tray as he finishes speaking.*)

Somewhere in this messed up mix . . . I mean, this mixed up mess . . . is the picture we chose . . . lost among all the others. All I need now is my magic bow to go with the arrow.

(*Pretends to pick up an imaginary bow. Steps far behind table. Pretends to thread arrow to invisible bow, to sight it and draw bow, but relaxes imaginary bowstring again without shooting arrow.*)

Maybe I'd better not. Because if I missed, the arrow would fly right out there where you are . . . and arrows never should be pointed where anybody is, should they? So all of you just pretend that I have a magic bow . . . Here comes the arrow . . . winging through the air.

(*Hurries forward with it. Steadies bag with other hand, pushes arrow tip through hole in card and back of bag, then right on out through front of bag. Holding up bag and arrow, secretly loosens card stuck to rear of bag. Looks toward first boy who took batch of cards.*)

Now what was that picture you gave me? Does anybody remember?

(*When they all shout that it was the tree, he holds the back end of the arrow firmly with right hand and, with left hand, grasps the bottom of the bag and rips the bag straight down and free of arrow. Reveals card impaled on it, back of which is still to audience.*)

Yes . . . that's right. It was the tree.

(*Removes card and slowly turns it around to show that it pictures the tree.*)

And the magic arrow has found its mark . . . shot by magic right through the mixed up mess into the tree you gave me!

(*Gathers things up, puts them into suitcase on chair, and starts next routine.*)

Cats and Canaries

EVERYBODY joins in this one which brings the show near its ending with a noisy romp of fun. Before it is over, they'll be shouting their lungs out, when they aren't howling like cats or whistling like canaries. All of which should leave them with a feeling that they have had a good time playing magical games with you.

For this game, you divide the entire audience into two teams, although they don't leave their seats to play it. Those seated to the left of the hall take the team name of "Cats," and those to the right are "Canaries." They make the appropriate noises and then become mixed up over whether you showed them a red handkerchief or a green one. You lead the teams to take sides, half the audience yelling it was red while the other half shouts that it was green. It finally ends in mutual laughter when you show that they all were right. The handkerchief is half red and half green.

The secret of the magic involved is one you already know. You use the cloth bag with two sections that you made for *The Little Black Bag*. That, plus two handkerchiefs and one special one, are the only props. Everything else depends on the order in which they are put into the bag and taken out, which requires a little practice to memorize, but otherwise leaves you free to concentrate on the presentation of the routine.

What you need:

Two green and two red 18″ square Japanese silk handkerchiefs and the help of someone with a sewing machine.

The cloth bag made as explained in *The Little Black Bag*.

How you make the props:

Cut one green and one red handkerchief in halves. Sew a red half to a green half with a seam down the middle to make what looks like a single handkerchief that is half red and half green.

How you use them:

Roll up the two-color handkerchief and put it into the bottom left corner of the rear section of the bag. Put the green one loosely on top of it in the same rear section. Now put the red one in the front section and everything is ready.

Here is the order in which you will take out the handkerchiefs and put them back:

Take the red handkerchief from the front section and show it to the "Cats" at the left side of the hall and then turn the front section inside out to show the bag empty. Turn the bag right side out again and put the red handkerchief in the front section where it was.

Go to the right side of the hall and remove the green handkerchief from the rear section of the bag. Show it to the "Canaries" and put it back into the rear section where it was without turning the bag inside out to show it empty.

Stand at the center a moment without taking anything from the bag.

Return to the right side of the hall and remove the red handkerchief from the front section and show it. Turn the front section of the bag inside out to show it empty and then turn it right side out again. Put the red handkerchief back into the front section where it was.

Go to the left side of the hall and remove the green handkerchief from the rear section. Show it, but don't turn the bag inside out. *This time, put the green one into the front section with the red one.*

Stand at the center, take the two-colored handkerchief from the rear section, and hold it stretched out between your hands. Then turn the rear section of the bag inside out and show it empty.

What you say and do:

MAGICIAN: (*Leads into this from previous routine. Stands at center as he speaks.*) For this magic game we're going to play, we need two teams. We'll choose up sides by dividing you down the center.

(*Holds up right arm and points to center aisle or direct center of room.*)

This is the dividing line right here. All of you on this side . . .

(*Sweeps arm to left.*)

. . .will be Cats. . . . And all of you on this side . . .

(*Sweeps arm to right.*)

. . . will be Canaries.

(*Goes to left.*)

Let's hear you sound like cats.

(*Waits for cat howls to die and goes to right.*)

Now let's hear everybody on this side whistle like canaries.
(*Waits for whistling to die down and points to an imaginary person in center.*)

Not you . . . you belong with the Cats. Whoever heard a cat whistle?

(*Laughs with them and returns to center.*)

Now to have fun with this game, each team is going to have to keep a secret from the other. All right now . . . everybody on this side . . .

(*Waves arm to right.*)

. . . all you Canaries, close your eyes tight. No fair peeking or you'll spoil the fun. Have you all got your eyes shut? Good. Don't open them until I tell you.

(*Picks up bag from table and goes to left.*)

Now I'm going to take something out of this little black bag I have and show it to all you Cats. The Canaries will have their turn in a minute. As you'll see there will be only one thing in the bag. What it is . . . that's your secret. Don't say a thing when I show it to you. Don't even whisper. Don't let them guess.

(*Turns head to right and looks in that direction.*)

All you Canaries over there . . . are your eyes still shut?

(*Doesn't make an issue of this since it makes little real difference whether some peek or not.*)

Now . . . Cats.

(*In silence, removes red handkerchief from bag, holds it up, shows bag empty, puts handkerchief back into bag.*)

All right, Canaries . . . you can open your eyes . . . Now this time, all of you Cats close your eyes. And I don't care if cats can see in the dark . . . you're not supposed to. Don't peek.

(*Goes to right.*)

It's your turn, Canaries. I'm going to show you something.

But don't call out what you see. This is your secret from the Cats.

(*Turns head to left and calls in that direction.*)

Eyes all closed, Cats? Play fair now . . . keep them closed until I say to open them.

(*Faces front.*)

Now . . . Canaries.

(*In silence, removes green handkerchief from bag, shows it and puts it back.*)

All right, Cats . . . open your eyes.

(*Goes to center.*)

Now when I count three . . . not before then, but when I count to three . . . all you Cats and Canaries together . . . just as loudly as you can . . . call out the color you saw. What color was it? One . . . two . . . three!

(*Waits for clamor to die. Smiles and coaxes second yell.*)

I'm sorry. I didn't hear that clearly. What color did you say it was?

(*Shakes head. Goes to right.*)

Just this side now . . . not you Cats, over there. Just Canaries. What color was it?

(*As they shout that it was green, he pulls red handkerchief from bag, shows bag empty and puts it back. Then hurries to left side.*)

What color did you say it was?

(*As they shout it was red, he pulls green handkerchief from bag, puts it back. Goes to center.*)

It sounds to me as if you all changed places. Are you Cats still where you were?

(*Looks to left.*)

Let's hear you sound like cats.

(*Waits for howls to quiet.*)

Well, you certainly don't sound like canaries. Maybe you swallowed the Canaries.

(*Looks to right.*)

Are you sure who you are? Let's hear you whistle like canaries.

(*When whistles die down.*)

Well, that much is straight. Let's all try it again. What color did you see? Everybody!

(*As they shout, he pulls two-colored handkerchief from bag, shows bag otherwise empty.*)

I guess that makes everybody right.

(*Smiles and holds handkerchief outstretched.*)

You were right all the time!

(*Puts handkerchief and bag into suitcase on chair. Immediately begins closing number.*)

John Q. Cottontail's Friend

YOU HAVE now brought your show to a peak of group excitement and all that remains is to provide a way of saying a pleasant good-by to your young friends. By tradition, most "kid shows" end with the production of a live rabbit. The use of a live animal, however, presents the average amateur magician with troublesome problems in the care and maintenance of such a pet, as well as in the transportation and the handling. Perhaps the best substitute is an ending that plays on the same theme, but with a surprise that supplies its own good reason for not pulling a rabbit from a hat.

In this one, you introduce a glove puppet rabbit, which you take from a hat shown otherwise empty. After a little by-play, you explain that magicians are always producing rabbits from hats and that you think it is only fair to try it the other way around for a change. So your puppet rabbit produces a magician from the hat that was just shown empty. The "magician" really is another glove puppet. With one on each hand, you have them thank the boys and girls and say good-by.

The magician puppet, folded small, has been hidden throughout your show behind an attractively decorated cardboard box that is covered with a lid. This box may be used to hold props for other routines. You rest the empty hat on top of the box and when you pick it up again your fingers secretly scoop the puppet into the hat so that John Q. Cottontail can produce his friend, the magician.

What you need:

A decorated cardboard box, about 5″ high.

A man's hat. If this is a top hat, so much the better, but any hat will do.

A rubber band.

The glove puppet rabbit. These are available in many toy stores.

A glove puppet magician. This you will have to make. Perhaps the easiest way is to adapt some other hand puppet. Visit a few places where toys are sold and try to find a puppet with a head that might be that of the magician. Cover the

JOHN Q. COTTONTAIL'S FRIEND

MAGICIAN GLOVE PUPPET

RABBIT GLOVE PUPPET

PROP BOX

AUDIENCE

Magician Puppet rolled up and fastened with RUBBER BAND

arms and body with black material that makes the glove part look like a small cape and sew a matchstick wand to one of the hands. Make a small top hat of a round piece of cardboard for the upper part and a flat one for the brim, both covered with adhesive-backed black felt, and draw it down far enough over the sides of the head so you can glue it firmly in place. If necessary, facial features can be altered by painting in tiny changes with a felt-tip marking pen. But there is no need to produce an elaborate figure. All you want is a puppet that will suggest the traditional image of the magician.

How you use them:

Fold up the magician puppet by bringing the arms together and then gathering the glove part and folding it to the left side of the head. Put the rubber band around it to hold it as a compact bundle. Rest this on the table directly

against the rear of the prop box. Have the hat, with the rabbit puppet inside it, brim upwards next to the box.

Pick up the hat with your right hand, fingers under the brim and thumb on top. With your left hand, take the rabbit puppet out of the hat and show it. Hold up the hat with your right hand and clearly show that it is empty. Casually put it brim down on top of the box, so that the brim extends a few inches over the rear edge of the box. Leave the hat there a moment.

Slip your left hand into the glove of the rabbit puppet, finger and thumb in the arms in the usual manner, and make the puppet wave, bow to the audience and so on. Keep the puppet on your left hand. With your right hand, reach to pick up the hat. Put your right fingers behind the box and get them under the hidden magician puppet. Slide it up against the rear of the box until it touches the hat. Close your thumb over the top edge of the brim and lift the hat from the rear, turning the crown of it toward the audience to let the puppet drop inside the hat, and then continuing to turn the hat over until it is brim upwards. This should look as if you just picked up the hat. But do it smoothly and deliberately, not as if you were in a hurry about it because you had something to hide.

Step away from the table, carrying the hat brim upwards, and transfer it to your left hand, which takes it at the brim with the finger and thumb that are in the arms of the rabbit puppet. Tilt the hat slightly toward yourself. Put your right hand inside and lift up the rubber band with your fingers. Press your thumb against the magician puppet and push it free of the rubber band. Lift your empty right hand out of the hat again, as if you were producing an imaginary rabbit from the hat.

This bit of business is necessary to release the folded magician puppet from the rubber band, so that when it finally is produced there will be no fumbling for it with your rabbit-gloved left hand. It is covered when performing the routine by the remark you make about magicians always pulling rabbits from hats and it should appear as if you were making a casual gesture suited to the words.

Now take the hat with your right hand. With your left, reach into it, and have the rabbit produce the magician. Put the hat on the table and then slip your right hand into the magician puppet and work the two of them, one puppet on each hand and with both hands held shoulder-high.

What you say and do:

MAGICIAN: Before I go, I'd like to show you a friend of mine.

(*Right hand picks up hat. Left hand takes out puppet. Does this quickly to avoid any false expectation that a real rabbit may be produced. Right hand rests hat on box.*)

His name is John Quincy Cottontail.

(*Puts puppet on left hand.*)

John Quincy, I'd like to introduce my friends.

(*Puppet turns head against magician's shoulder.*)

He's bashful. Come on, John Quincy . . . don't be embarrassed.

(*Puppet looks around timidly, shivers, quickly ducks head against shoulder again.*)

Oh, for goodness' sake . . . you're acting as scared as a rabbit.

(*Looks to audience.*)

Maybe if you said hello to him first . . . if all of you said, "Hello, John Quincy Cottontail . . ."

(*Coaxes them to call out. Puppet turns, waves, claps hands, waves again.*)

That's better. I told you they were all your friends.

(*Right hand picks up hat, secretly loading magician puppet, and transfers it to left hand so rabbit puppet holds it.*)

Magicians are forever producing rabbits from hats . . .

(*Right hand goes into hat, thumbs magician puppet free of rubber band, immediately comes out empty, making gesture of pulling rabbit from hat.*)

Since turnabout is only fair play . . . I thought for a change I'd do something different.

(*Takes hat with right hand.*)

Instead of a magician pulling a rabbit from a hat . . . John Quincy Cottontail is going to produce a magician from the hat.

(*Rabbit puppet waves arms over top of hat, looks down into it, ducks down fast and slowly lifts magician puppet into view. Right hand puts hat aside on table, then slips into glove of magician puppet with help of left.*)

Thank all our friends for being such a good audience and tell them you hope they've had some fun.

(*Hands hold puppets high. Both puppets applaud the audience and then wave to it as magician starts exit. He stops, faces front, and smiles. Bows to audience as puppets also bow.*)

Thank you. You've been swell to help me do my magic. I've enjoyed meeting you all.

(*Exits with puppets waving good-by, or if not on a platform, he returns to stand beside suitcase, puppets waving for a moment.*

Good-by. . . .

(*Curtains close, or he puts puppets into suitcase and shuts the lid.*)

The Kid Show Set-up

WHEN you have to put on your "kid show" in a place where there are no curtains, one of your problems will be in setting things up for it. If you do this in full view, youngsters will stand around to watch and ask all sorts of eager questions. They will want to find out how the tricks are done if they can, but that natural curiosity is only part of it. A magician is someone very special to younger children. More than anything, they want to become his friends if he will give them that chance. He cannot be stern or impatient. At the same time, he has to keep the situation under control or he will never get things ready for the show.

He should try to arrange with those in charge for a separate room he can use, or even a large closet. He then can put things together with some privacy and set his props in order in the bottom of his suitcase. Then, just before he is to appear, and after the youngsters have taken their seats, he can carry out the suitcase as if it were a large tray and put it on a chair that has its back to the audience. Things that should be in view on the table at the start of the show can be removed from the suitcase and placed there. Other props may be left in the suitcase until he is ready to use them in the performance. The open lid of the suitcase will help to screen his hands and allow for any last-minute arrangement of props.

On a chair at the other side of the table, he will have a second suitcase. This is empty at the start of the show. As he finishes with the things for each trick, they go into the second suitcase. When the show is over, he just closes the lid, snaps it shut, and has no worries about the youngsters who crowd around. The second suitcase can be packed before the show with slip-over chair covers, a table cover, a fold-flat waste basket and anything else he may decide to use to dress up his setting. After the show, they are then packed into the first suitcase, which has been emptied by then.

Even with these precautions, however, there will be times before a show when boys and girls do give him little privacy. The best way to handle the problem is to enlist their help, which they will be eager to give. He can ask if they will do him a favor and put the slipcovers on the chairs, or if they will get him a glass of water or a piece of paper, perform any little errand that will lead them away for a few moments while he takes care of some secret set-up that must be made.

In addition to the two chairs and two suitcases, he will need a center table, which can be either a card table or a magic table of his own. If he is performing on a level with his audience, rather than on a platform, he will want to keep the young ones from crowding so close there is no room left for him to show his magic. He can't very well command the audience to move back or to change seats. Instead, when first setting things up, he can put his table about four feet in front of where he really wants it. Then, after they have all taken their places and just before he starts the show, he can move the table back and he will have plenty of room in which to perform.

CURTAIN CALL

Stretching the Show

IN THE days of vaudeville, there was a saying that a performer should always end his act so as to leave the audience wanting more. It is still a wise one for any magician to follow. Knowing when to quit is one of the more important things he can learn. As a general rule, if he is invited to perform on a program that will include other entertainment, an act of from ten to fifteen minutes is long enough. If he is to be the only entertainer, he usually should plan to put on a half-hour show.

There are times, however, when he may want to stretch one of the shows a little or substitute a different routine for one that doesn't seem to suit the occasion. Many of the routines given in this book can be adapted from one type of show to another. Having learned them, he will be able to add material that already has been practiced and rehearsed without having to work out something entirely new.

Among the routines he might add to a club show are these: *A Trip to the Orient, The Instant Shopper, A Visit from Houdini, All the Rice in China,* and *Let's Go to the Fair.* If he watches the back angles, he could include *Hawaiian Magic,* or if there are children present, substitute for it, *Jump for Joy.*

His stage show can be stretched by adding *Under Your Spell, The Instant Shopper, Fast and Slow* and *The Magic Tax,* if there are steps that will let him go down into the audience for the latter and his stay there is brief.

He might add these to his *Magic In A Briefcase: Under Your Spell,* and *A Visit to the Orient.*

For the "kid show," he can arrange ahead of time to give some boy in the audience his handkerchief and then borrow it back to perform *Who's Worried Now?* If he leaves out *Cats and Canaries,* he can substitute *The Little Black Bag* for it, but he can't have both in the same program since they use the same basic prop. *The Bewildered Milkman* also would be entertaining for young children, who would enjoy seeing the milk containers turn upside down. Other routines he might include are: *Under Your Spell* and *All the Rice in China.* But with the "kid show" especially, he should be careful not to make the program too long.

You should do your own timing once you have a show set the way you want it. Have someone clock each routine, not at rehearsal, but during several actual performances and then figure an average. That way you will know how much to cut or stretch to meet the needs of any occasion. Work out any changes you want to make on paper, weighing the effect of each routine, the type of magic involved, and where you will place it in the show so as to keep a good balance and avoid having two similar effects follow one another. Plan such changes ahead of time, not right before the show.

It is smart, though, to carry an extra routine or two in your suitcase, to be prepared in case something happens to one of your props or you find it impossible to do a certain trick because of the performing conditions. You also may be asked to stretch a show at the last minute because the entertainment plans have been changed or some other performer has failed to show up. But the routines you carry should be those you have rehearsed and you should know exactly where you will fit them into the show.

Cutting a show generally is easier than stretching it. Usually you will want to keep your opening and closing routines and your next-to-closing feature, and then eliminate less important ones in between. If you have timed your routines individually, you can trim any show almost to the minute.

Building Your Own Routines

THERE are two good starting points for building new routines of your own. One is to decide on some magical plot or effect you want to produce and then work out the simplest possible method of achieving it. The other is to take some standard trick or prop and figure out a use for it that will illustrate a good magical theme. Remember that any trick or method only has value in proportion to the entertainment that can be woven around it. The cleverest trick in the world is useless to the entertaining magician without some clothing of imagination to cover its bare bones.

A magician is judged, not by the tricks he does, but by how well he uses them to entertain. He is an actor in a fantasy planned to appeal to the imagination. People don't believe he really is a magician, any more than they believe in the reality of Santa Claus or Peter Pan. But if he plans his routines entertainingly, they will be willing to pretend with him that it might be fun if there were such a thing as magic, even while they are smiling at what logically is nonsense. In a way, a magic show is something like a science fiction story or a good detective mystery. People know that what is happening isn't so, but it is fun just the same to be surprised by the unusual or to try to solve the mystery.

Well-planned routines heighten that enjoyment. The showmanship you bring to them is like the gift wrapping around a present which stimulates the imagination so that what is inside the package will be better enjoyed. In working them out, try to eliminate unnecessary words and gestures. Verbal by-play and humor have a good place in presentation, but needless movement and aimless chatter do not. Plan your movements and gestures so they seem natural and graceful. Plot them so that when you pick up something from a table, for instance, you don't turn your back to do it. Back a few steps and then approach the object from the side.

Despite the old saying that "the hand is quicker than the eye," there are hardly any tricks that depend on the speed of the hand for accomplishment. Quick movements, instead of hiding things, draw attention to them. As a general rule, it is wise to make your hand movements slowly and deliberately. Think out your routines to decide whether you should hold something a moment longer to make sure the idea you want to put across really registers with the audience, whether everybody has a clear view of what you are doing, and if a gesture you are making really directs attention to what you want people to see.

All of magic is built around what is called "misdirection." Simply put, it means directing the attention of the audience away from some object or some action that must be kept secret. The magician knows, for instance, that anything in motion usually attracts attention, so he plans his routine to keep something hidden in a hand that remains perfectly still while his other hand moves away. He gazes intently at the hand that is empty and the audience looks there, too.

Sometimes he misdirects attention with a quick turn of the head, a sharp exclamation, an upward glance. All these things are planned distractions. Whenever there is a secret move to be made, something should be planned to draw attention from it and focus it somewhere else. An audience usually will look in the direction a magician looks. Their eyes will follow his. It is his business as a magician to plan his routines so as to lead the attention of his audience in the direction he wishes it to take.

Misdirection may be verbal rather than visual. By his talk, the magician leads the thoughts of the audience away from the truth. His words are chosen to plant some idea he wants them to accept. He may lead them to expect one thing to happen and then show that something entirely different has happened. With a joke or witty remark, he may cause them to laugh at a planned moment so that their minds won't be on what he is doing secretly. Sound can play a part in misdirection, too, as it does in *The Magic Tax*, when the hidden coins falling into the bucket seem to be those the magician is dropping from his hand. Many props are built to provide misdirection in themselves because of their construction.

Your talk should be learned from a written script, just as if you were learning a part in a play. It should be worked over, cut, changed around, pointed up, and studied for timing and delivery. Pauses should be marked, inflections noted, tones of voice decided upon. Remember that you are acting, that your voice needs comedy, drama, the effective use of silences, and that most of all, that you should get into the character and really feel the part of the magician you are playing.

A good rule to follow is never to depart from your written script during a show. There will be times, of course, when things happen that may make some off-handed remark neces-sary. But it takes a master entertainer of long experience to make impromptu talk interesting. As you give shows, you will find you want to change things here and there, perhaps insert a joke or some patter to cover a bit of business that seems to drag. There may be parts of a new routine that don't go over at all. Make a mental note of the changes, write them in, practice them, and then try them at the next show you give. But don't be tempted to change the lines while perform-ing. If you start making up things to say, you can easily get out of character or wander away from the plot. Aside from that, knowing exactly what you will say and do is as impor-tant to the pace and smoothness of your performance as it is to your own self-confidence.

Many of the props in this book have utility uses. Some of them already have been briefly suggested. Here are other ways of using them that may give you ideas for new routines:

Under Your Spell—With the tube made for this, you can produce, vanish or change silk handkerchiefs, ribbon, rope or anything else of reasonable size and weight that will fit into it. You might cover the black construction paper with a highway map, tell how you were stranded in your car at night miles from a filling station, and produce a toy gas pump. By using the same tube and giving the hidden section a solid cardboard bottom instead of the one it has, you could switch the plot around and tell about an old prospector who found gold, and pour from it a stream of glittering gold powder. In the form of a school graduation diploma, the tube could be shown empty and then your "graduation present" of a wrist watch could be produced from it.

Fast and Slow—The folder constructed for this also will vanish and change other things, but they have to be rather flat ones or those that may be compressed. By using the same principle, but making up the folder in a larger size in the form of a restaurant menu, you might put an empty paper napkin into it and have it appear with a thin sandwich wrapped in the napkin. Instead of a menu, the folder might be made in the form of two BEWARE OF THE DOG signs hinged together, without any slot across the face of it. You could show a large picture of a dog, slide it into the back, and take out a previously hidden picture of a cat that "chased the dog away."

The Little Black Bag—You have already seen how this prop was adapted to use in *Cats and Canaries* for an entirely different effect. Its other uses are many. Again, you can produce, vanish or change things with it. You can force the selection of cards, colors, pictures or other things by having a number of duplicates of one card or other object hidden in the rear section, showing all different ones and dropping them in the front, and then holding the bag open to the rear for a person to dip his hand in and take out what must be one of the duplicates you wish to force.

The Orange Swindle—Instead of the orange that comes off the red ribbons, you might use a small model of a doll house with a hole through the center so as to thread the ribbons through it and tie them. Then tell of a magician who was elected to Congress, how an important housing bill was held up by red tape, and the way he used his magic to free it and get it passed.

The Magic Tax—A different magical theme for a "kid show" would be to play a game of *Button, Button, Who's Got the Button?* Instead of pulling coins from the air, you would produce buttons. You might magically collect sticks of chewing gum, small wrapped candies, or toy sheriff's badges. For adults, the bucket would let you pull old political campaign buttons, cigarette lighters, or door keys from the air.

No Soap—The principle of using a small lead weight to produce the sound of something solid, also employed in *Where's the Wand?*, is one that can be adapted to many things magical. A drinking glass covered with a piece of paper to which a tiny weight is attached might have the paper pressed around it in such a way as to outline the shape of the glass. Then the glass itself secretly could be slid from the paper into a hat. But when the paper was tapped on a table, it would sound as if the glass were still in it. A moment later, the paper could be crushed and torn apart, the glass having vanished.

The Feast of Lanterns—By finding a small rubber ball the proper size to jam into the mouth of the hidden cup so as to seal it, a magical beach resort plot might be developed. The bottom part of the bucket would be filled with water and a few large ornamental sea shells. Then sand could be shown and poured into the smaller cup, the rubber ball displayed as one that was found on the beach and placed into the bucket so it squeezed into the smaller cup and sealed it, and a toy sand shovel used to pretend you were mixing the sand. Water would be poured out of the bucket as the first surprise, then the sea shells could be produced, still convincingly wet, and finally the ball could be discovered again and the sand poured out of the bucket, still dry.

The Instant Shopper—For an adult audience, the financial pages of a newspaper could be used and dollar bills or dummy shares of "oil stock" produced. For children, a comic sheet could be loaded with objects representing the various comic strip characters, things such as a hair ribbon, a toy wrist watch, a dog leash, and one of those wind-up sets of chattering false teeth that are sold in novelty shops.

Blue Ribbon Magic—The double cardboard folder, with the side that locks to keep hidden whatever is put into it because of its seal of double-stick tape will serve many of the uses of a standard prop magicians call a "card box." It will vanish or change ribbons, cards, slips of paper, theater or sports tickets, a borrowed dollar bill, trading stamps, a coin, key or business card.

A Visit from Houdini—The principle of deliberately displaying the flap from the slate as a sign put up in full view of the audience is a bold swindle that might be used to make a photo appear in a picture frame. The "flap" could be a piece of glass with a cardboard backing sheet. When in place, to cover a picture previously hidden in the frame itself, it would make the frame seem empty. The other side of the flap would be a sign of some sort, worded so as to tie in with the magical story you tell.

Jump for Joy—The large bag held together with double-stick tape will accomplish some rather startling vanishes by the sudden exposure of its entire inside. If a large enough bag is used, some rather bulky objects can be made to disappear. Such a bag would vanish a small child's dress, a duplicate of which might be found in another such bag on a hanger previously shown without it. The hanger with the dress on it would be in the front part of the second bag from the start, and an empty hanger shown and dropped into the rear part. Things like imitation packages of meat and vegetables could be made to vanish during a "magical shopping trip." If the bag were sturdy enough, Cinderella's slipper might disappear from it, so that the magician's fantasy could place it into the hands of Prince Charming.

These are examples of some of the ideas that props such as those in this book might inspire for building new routines. There are other books of magic with hundreds of other tricks to serve as starting places. The tricks are unimportant. All that counts is what you make of them. Use your imagination in the same way you ask your audiences to imagine you are a magician. If you *really* were a magician, what would you do, what would you wish, what dreams, desires or amusing happenings would you make come true?

You can't really do it. But you can pretend, you can make believe, and in doing so find all the plots you will ever need for new and fresh magical themes, so that others will want to make believe with you and enjoy the fun that comes, not from watching tricks, but from seeing magic.